A Treatise on War Inflation

*Publications of the
Bureau of Business and Economic Research
University of California*

A Treatise on War Inflation

*Present Policies and Future
Tendencies in the United States*

BY

WILLIAM FELLNER

UNIVERSITY OF CALIFORNIA PRESS
BERKELEY AND LOS ANGELES
1942

UNIVERSITY OF CALIFORNIA PRESS
BERKELEY, CALIFORNIA

◆

CAMBRIDGE UNIVERSITY PRESS
LONDON, ENGLAND

COPYRIGHT, 1942, BY
THE REGENTS OF THE UNIVERSITY OF CALIFORNIA

Foreword

THE FOLLOWING *study by William Fellner, Assistant Professor of Economics in the University of California, is the first of a series of research studies conducted under the auspices of the Bureau of Business and Economic Research of the University. The Bureau was organized in July, 1941, to promote and assist research in economics and business by members of the University faculty. The Bureau is under the general direction of a presidential committee, consisting at present of the following members of the Department of Economics: Professors J. B. Condliffe (chairman), Stuart Daggett,* Howard S. Ellis, E. T. Grether, and Paul S. Taylor.*

The opinions expressed in this study are those of the author. The functions of the Bureau of Business and Economic Research are confined to facilitating the prosecution of independent scholarly research by members of the faculty.

FRANK L. KIDNER,
Director.

---

* Appointed June 1, 1942, replacing Professor R. A. Gordon, on leave of absence to government service.

Preface

THIS VOLUME results from a study undertaken for the Bureau of Business and Economic Research at the University of California from October, 1941, to May, 1942. I am indebted to Mr. Lawrence Klein for the ability, judgment, and effort he contributed during the entire period of the study, and to Miss Virginia Galbraith for the apt and valuable assistance which she provided for several months.

Chapter i of the volume attempts a brief general analysis of the causes of war inflation. Chapters ii to vi, inclusive, are concerned with contemporary economic problems, mainly with problems of the American war economy. Chapters ii and iii discuss "real" aspects; chapters iv and v concentrate more on monetary and fiscal relationships. Chapter vi discusses present policies and attempts to appraise future developments. A brief discussion of occurrences between May and October, 1942, is contained in a Postscript. It is recommended that readers interested only in the general character of the problem rather than in detailed factual analysis omit chapters ii to v, inclusive. It is hoped that chapters i and vi may be of some use for students, too.

The numerous suggestions and the detailed criticism made by Professor Howard S. Ellis were of great help. Professors Stuart Daggett, Frank L. Kidner, Sanford A. Mosk, and Earl R. Rolph made several valuable suggestions. I wish to express my sincere thanks also for the helpful comments of Mrs. Mary Mosk.

W. F.

Berkeley, October, 1942

Contents

CHAPTER	PAGE
I. The Irrationality of War Finance	1

Rational war finance—The justified degree of monetary expansion—Nonexpansionary borrowing—Redundant income and direct controls—The inflation potential and the postwar period—Direct controls and the progressiveness of taxation—The basic cause of war inflation—The effectiveness of inflation control—Summary

II. The Stimulus to Civilian Production in the Period of Nonbelligerency 22

Induced consumption and induced investment—Past "gain" and future effort

III. The Real Burden of the War 41

The consumption level and the war program—Professor Pigou's four categories—Numerical comparisons: changes in distribution—Numerical comparisons: changes in physical composition—Other factors affecting appraisal of future burden

IV. The Financing of Defense Prior to Pearl Harbor 61

Expansionary financing vs. induced consumption and induced investment—The first fiscal year—The second fiscal year—The early part of the third fiscal year—The behavior of velocity

V. Noninflationary War Finance 79

Could inflation tendencies be completely avoided in a major war?—The general case for income taxes—Expansionary financing—Excises—Borrowing from voluntary savings: corporate income taxes—Borrowing from depreciation and liquidation funds—Should the savings be borrowed, or should saving merely offset borrowing?—Compulsory individual saving—Individual income taxes—Deduction at the source—The potentiality of declining average productivity

VI. Present Policies—Future Potentialities . . . 111

The nature of the difficulties—Actual policies of war finance—Weaknesses of controlled inflation: future potentialities

Postscript on Recent Developments 148

Contents

APPENDIX | PAGE

I. Tables 155

II. Charts 169

    Publications Used 173

    Index 179

CHAPTER I

The Irrationality of War Finance

● *Rational war finance.*—The problem of raising money for the purposes of war finance is inherently different from the problem of mobilizing real resources for a war. In a major war, real resources—labor, plant, equipment, raw materials—inevitably become scarce. Money becomes scarce only if policies are pursued which will make it scarce. It is clearly desirable to overcome the scarcity of real resources so far as is possible, but it is clearly undesirable to make money more and more abundant: abundance of money in relation to commodities and services reduces the efficiency of the war economy and establishes a highly inequitable distribution of the war burden. To avoid making money abundant in relation to real goods is one of the main objectives of reasonable war finance.

One should not be misled into the belief, however, that the appropriate policies of war finance are capable alone of producing an efficient war economy and of distributing the burden of a major war with equity. To achieve these objectives, certain direct controls must be required, even if rational persons are free to choose those policies of finance which seem justified. Yet the scope of the necessary controls would be narrower and their effectiveness greater if war finance were strictly rational. Modern warfare renders it necessary to introduce direct controls on a very extensive scale and to enforce them with a huge apparatus, largely because strictly rational policies of war finance are politically not "feasible." Moreover, the controls are not merely more extensive, but also less effective because of their extensiveness.

Rationality in war finance would call for preventing the formation of redundant disposable money incomes. Incomes after taxes are redundant in this sense if the public tends to spend on consumption amounts that cannot be spent without exerting an upward pressure on the price level.[1] Redundant income creates what may be called an inflation potential or latent inflation. "Controlled inflation" is typically a mixture of latent and actual inflation, that is, of a controlled inflation potential and a more or less controlled inflationary process. If under the pressure of redundant income prices actually start to spiral upward, the distribution of the war burden becomes entirely fortuitous, and at the same time it becomes exceedingly difficult to prevent resources from flowing out of the war sector of the economy into the civilian sector. The authorities may attempt to keep redundant incomes from being spent on consumers' goods by means of rationing and price control. Yet, if the pressure of redundant income is substantial, these controls are unlikely to be completely effective during the war; and since after the war the controls cannot be maintained indefinitely, the excess money is likely to produce inflationary phenomena in the postwar period. A strictly rational policy of war finance would avoid the creation of redundant income.

This means that if rational statesmen were free to choose whatever policies should seem to them justified, they would tax at a substantially higher rate than is usual in time of war. They would presumably not tax at a rate which would be high enough to balance the budget without a residual, but they would tax at a rate which would not be much lower than that required to balance the wartime budget.

---

[1] This statement might suggest that "inflation" occurs whenever total money income rises more (or declines less) than total real output. This, in fact, is one of the possible definitions of inflation. Yet it should be pointed out that certain characteristics of the "inflationary process" arise as a consequence of a discrepancy between total money income and real output only if it is not accompanied by a decline in physical output per unit of factor input. Only in this event do money earnings per unit of factor input increase. I prefer to define "inflation" so as to exclude price changes accompanied by changes in physical productivity. It is implied in the text that the discrepancy between changes in money income and changes in real output, characteristic of war economies, is not typically accompanied by declining physical productivity of factor inputs.

The justified degree of monetary expansion.—So long as the real output flow is still increasing, some amount of monetary expansion seems desirable. This consideration would justify raising some fraction of the war fund by borrowing money from the banking system. The proposition may be given numerical content with reference to the present American situation, which, however, in this introductory chapter is referred to merely for the sake of illustration. If, for example, in the present American circumstances the stock of money were rising at an annual rate of 10 per cent, this would hardly generate an inflationary pressure. The total physical output flow of the American economy has been increasing much less rapidly since the summer of 1941 than previously, because since the summer of 1941 the growth of the defense industries has been associated with a decline in the civilian sector; nevertheless, aggregate real output is still rising. It is true that the new money (i.e., the additional amount of check deposits) which comes into existence when the government borrows from banks would have to be prevented from becoming additional demand for consumers' goods, for while the aggregate supply of goods is still rising the supply of consumers' goods is already declining. But this only means that once the public should have earned the increased money incomes corresponding to the additional borrowing from banks, tax liabilities would have to be increased, and income taxes would have to be withheld at the source, so as to force the public to pay the additional money back to the Treasury rather than spend it on consumption. In other words, the public should be forced, in circumstances like these, to "spend" the entire increase in money incomes[2] on taxes rather than on consumers' goods. This would be true even if the supply of consumers' goods should remain stable while the supply of all goods increased. As things stand, the supply

---

[2] In principle one should say, "The increase in money incomes minus the additional savings," but it will be argued that in the event of noninflationary war finance individual savings would presumably become negligible.

of consumers' goods is declining, and consequently tax deductions at the source would have to be higher than the increase in money income. But all this does not imply that money income should be completely prevented from rising so long as the aggregate physical output flow, including the output of the war sector, is expanding.

There is a difference between (*a*) letting money incomes rise and taxing the increase away, and (*b*) not letting money incomes rise.[3] In the first case, additional money has been spent on certain goods (in the given circumstances, on war materials) when the additional incomes have been earned; in the second, the total flow of money spending is stabilized. In the first case, the increasing government expenditures are balanced with future tax revenues, that is, they are less than balanced with present tax revenues; in the second, "present" expenditures and "present" tax revenues balance continuously. Complete stabilization of money incomes in times of rising real output exercises an undesirable downward pressure on prices.

Returning, for the sake of illustration, to present American circumstances, a downward pressure on the price level could presumably be avoided if government borrowing from banks should increase the stock of money, including check deposits, by roughly 5 to 6 billions a year. This would roughly correspond to a 10-per cent rise of the money stock. Yet if aside from this increase the government should have to raise the entire war fund by taxation, then the tax revenue of the fiscal year ending in June, 1943, would have to come close to 70 billions. Would a strictly rational war-finance policy attempt to raise a tax revenue of this magnitude? Not quite; but such a policy might well attempt to raise, by taxation, about 55 billions out of a national income (at factor costs) of about 120 billions.

Generally speaking, intelligent financing of the advanced stages of a major war would require raising much the greater

---

[3] For a discussion of different aspects of this problem I am indebted to my colleagues, Professors Sanford A. Mosk and Earl R. Rolph.

part of the war fund by taxation. Some borrowing from banks is justified so long as aggregate real output is expanding; and some borrowing out of the current stream of savings is justified. The rest of the money requirement would have to be yielded by the tax system.

Nonexpansionary borrowing.—The savings on which noninflationary war finance could draw would mainly be those of corporate enterprise. Paradoxical as this may sound, inflationary war finance may rely rather heavily on the savings of individual income recipients whereas noninflationary war finance would not be in a position to do so. The degree of taxation which would be required to prevent money income from rising at a rate exceeding the rate of increase of physical output would reduce individual savings to insignificance. This is true especially if most of the taxation were progressive. In this event, the required degree of taxation might even generate a tendency to dissave, that is, to draw on old assets, since a relatively large share of the saving is normally undertaken by the higher brackets whereas dissaving is of frequent occurrence in the lowest income groups. The individual savings from which the usual type of war finance can borrow part of its requirements are mainly a product of inflationary war finance, that is, of one which creates an inflation potential. It does not prevent money incomes from rising in relation to real output. It does not tax at a rate sufficient to achieve this objective. Part of the excess money tends to be saved by the individual income recipient, especially if rationing and price control place obstacles in the way of consumption spending. The government is then capable of borrowing rather substantial amounts from current individual savings. Yet these savings merely diminish the existing inflationary pressure. In order to be diminished by individual savings the inflationary pressure has first to come into existence, and only to some limited extent will it be diminished by this process. If consumers, after having paid their taxes, are left with incomes which merely suffice to buy a substantially reduced flow of consumers' goods at market prices, they are unlikely to save any substantial part of their disposable incomes. With the tax structure progressive, they are even likely in the aggregate to dissave. Saving out of individual incomes will acquire significance only if the consumer is left with more income than is spendable at controlled prices on a controlled supply of consumers' goods. Part of these induced savings will be used to purchase government securities or will be hoarded, and to this extent the monetary pressure against which the controls have to work will be diminished. But these savings essentially are by-products of inflationary war finance. They are characteristic of what usually is called "controlled inflation."

The current savings of corporate enterprise would not necessarily, however, be eliminated by a policy attempting to confine itself to noninflationary methods. Corporations, even if taxed very heavily, do not spend their incomes after taxes on consumption. They may pay dividends out of these net incomes, or they may accumulate undistributed profits, that is, net corporate savings. The dividend payments become consumer incomes; the undistributed profits do not. Heavy wartime taxation of individual incomes stimulates the accumulation of net corporate savings which are not subject to individual income taxes, and this tendency may be strengthened by a legal limitation of dividend payments. If the investment of these net savings into civilian industries is rendered impossible by priorities and by the direct allocation of resources to war production, the corresponding funds become potentially available for the purpose of war finance. Moreover, in total war, priorities and allocations also impose a certain amount of capital consumption on the civilian industries. Certain industries are forced to liquidate their inventories, and others to defer replacements of plant and equipment. Hence the funds out of which noninflationary borrowing may occur exceed the current flow of net corporate savings by the current additions to unused depreciation and liquidation reserves.

In the conditions, for example, which may be expected to prevail in this country during the fiscal year 1942–43, gross corporate savings, that is, net corporate savings plus capital consumption, may well approximate 10 billions. This is the reason why a strictly rational war finance policy might, in these circumstances, attempt to raise somewhat more than 55 billions by taxation. Including the borrowing from gross corporate savings and some borrowing from banks, a total amount of 70 billions or slightly more could be obtained. The annual expenditures of the Treasury are now expected to exceed 70 billions by a slight margin. It should be added that the "borrowing from gross corporate savings" might partly appear in the form of such additional borrowing from banks, over and above the 5–6 billions previously mentioned, as is offset by new hoarding out of gross corporate earnings.

Redundant income and direct controls.—It is important to realize that the mere avoidance of inflationary fiscal policies would not of itself solve the two main problems of a war economy. To assure the required flow of war materials and of war services, and to distribute the economic war burden in an equitable manner, are the two prime objectives of wartime economic policy. In a major war these two objectives could not be achieved without direct controls even if it were possible to tax the public at exceedingly high rates.

Even should inflationary borrowing be completely avoided, certain scarce resources would still have to be allocated to the war industries by the means of direct government interference. The government of a nation waging total war could not afford to compete with the consumer for certain scarce resources even if it kept civilian buying power at a low level. Competition with the civilian sector would result in a distribution of these resources between the two sectors of the economy, whereas the entire supply of certain resources must be directed into the war sector. Assume, for example, that the government of the United States were to require for its annual expenditures a fund corresponding to 60 per cent of the national income at factor costs (which seems a realistic assumption) and that it could raise most of this fund by means of taxation (which, of course, is an unrealistic assumption). Such a fiscal policy would not of itself assure the allocation of the entire available supply of rubber or of aluminum to the war sector of the economy. The public whose buying power would be seriously curtailed might not want to buy many rubber articles or many commodities containing aluminum, yet it still would tend to consume more rubber and more aluminum than can be made available for civilian purposes if the American war economy is to be efficient.

For the very same reason it is impossible to establish an equitable distribution of the war burden purely by means of fiscal policies. The prices of certain scarce commodities would tend to rise very sharply even at such low levels of total consumers' buying power. The general price level might conceivably be kept down by over-all fiscal and monetary policies, but the prices of certain goods could not be prevented from rising substantially by these methods alone. In a war economy relative price movements should not be entirely excluded from the mechanism by which demand is directed away from fields of relative scarcity into fields of relative abundance. Yet, if the war burden is to be distributed in an equitable manner it is impossible to rely exclusively on relative price movements in the limitation of the demand for scarce essentials. Exclusive reliance on relative price changes might mean that certain "basic necessaries of life" would become available to the wealthy groups of the population only. The wartime demand for common foodstuffs, for example, should obviously not be limited by the same mechanism which in normal times limits the demand for luxuries.

Keeping down the aggregate buying power of the public would not obviate the necessity of allocating certain resources to war producers, nor of rationing scarce "necessaries of life" and controlling their prices. Moreover, it should be remembered that a policy avoiding all inflationary borrowing would not necessarily avoid all indirect inflationary phenomena. Noninflationary war finance fails of its purpose, even with respect to the curtailment of "total buying power," to the extent to which consumers dishoard under the impact of severe taxation. Consumer credit and private borrowing from banks would also contribute to the maintenance of consumption spending, if controls were not applied to the credit mechanism. It is obvious, therefore, that direct controls are indispensable if the two main objectives of a modern war economy—efficiency and equity—are to be realized to a reasonable degree. But it remains just as obvious that it would be much easier to achieve these objectives if the monetary pressure originating from redundant incomes could be eliminated. All controls aim at keeping down civilian purchases. They would be necessary even if taxation should curtail *total* buying power severely, because *certain* expenditures would still tend to be maintained at too high a level. But this circumstance does not justify policies leading to a sharp increase in disposable money incomes (after taxes) in times when the available supply of consumers' goods declines sharply. The excess money accumulating under such a policy cannot fail to reduce the effectiveness of the controls, and at the same time it constitutes a serious postwar menace.

The inflation potential and the postwar period.—Arguments which are intended to prove that the excess money income of war periods has an economic right to exist are unconvincing. These arguments frequently recognize the claim that redundant income arising from war finance is a postwar menace, but hold it to be incomplete and place the emphasis on the potentiality of deflationary developments in the postwar period. Or, it is argued that the earning of redundant income is an economic incentive to the income recipient since his buying power on the postwar market becomes correspondingly higher.

As to the first of these two arguments, it seems realistic to assume that in certain stages of the postwar process public policy will have to be directed toward the maintenance of money income and of money spending. But it does not seem realistic to assume that the temporarily frozen consumer incomes of the war period will tend to produce expansionary effects just at the right time and just in the right degree. The inflation potential accumulated during war periods typically tends to be unloaded in an early stage of postwar developments, at a time when the productive capacity of the civilian industries is still insufficient. Gradual rather than immediate abandonment of wartime controls may dampen the ensuing fluctuations, but here again the inflationary methods of war finance generate tendencies which an elaborate system of direct controls can at best only partly offset. The enforcement of postwar controls is even more difficult than that of wartime regulations since the attitude of the public toward measures of this kind is apt to become less favorable once the external menace to the nation is removed. It would be hard to justify the view that the future problems of the postwar economy can be well handled by creating and suppressing a huge inflation potential during the war and by releasing this potential afterward in the appropriate installments. Expansionary monetary and fiscal policies should be started at the time when they seem desirable, and they should be carried to the point which then seems appropriate.

It is unlikely, furthermore, that the maintenance of economic incentives would truly require the creation of excess money incomes during the war period. In normal circumstances marginal tax rates do have an important bearing on the economic incentive to increased effort. That percentage of a potential increase in money income which goes into increased tax payments may be defined as the marginal tax rate. Excessive marginal rates would, in normal circumstances, weaken or conceivably eliminate the economic incentive to efficiency. If a high share of total income is to be taxed away by income taxes, and if the lowest income brackets are to be exempt or leniently taxed, then marginal rates must approximate 100 per cent in the high brackets. So far as individual income taxation is concerned, it seems unlikely, however, that high wartime marginal rates, if confined to the upper brackets, would reduce economic efficiency or even that they would prevent a rise in efficiency. Upper-middle incomes and high incomes are mainly earned by persons whose future peacetime earnings will be substantially influenced by their "record" or "professional standing," and these latter typically improve when the earners move into a higher gross-income class even if the higher income before taxes leaves them, for the time being, with only a small amount of additional income after taxes. Moreover, in regions of the income structure where marginal tax rates would otherwise become excessive, compulsory lending (i.e., postwar credits) could be combined with taxation proper and this might contribute to keeping marginal rates at some distance below 100 per cent. At the same time it would also be possible to alleviate the long-run burden upon the low brackets by substituting compulsory loans for part of their tax burden,[4] although the dangers of postwar inflation do set certain limits to the total of postwar credits which may reasonably be accorded. Income taxation combined with some amount of compulsory lending is the method of war finance best suited to satisfy the requirements of equity, and it seems unlikely that considerations relating to efficiency would force a rational policy to refrain from heavy reliance on this method.[5]

Risk of reduced efficiency is higher if taxation becomes quasi-confiscatory on the corporate margin than if marginal rates become high for upper-bracket individual incomes. Unless increased efficiency means somewhat higher profits after taxes, the corporation will not typically be the better off on its post-

---

[4] This is the essence of the Keynes plan.
[5] Deduction at the source would, however, be essential, as was pointed out.

war market the more efficiently it produces war materials during the emergency. There is not much analogy between individuals and enterprises in this respect. It seems more likely that efficiency might suffer from marginal corporate tax rates approximating 100 per cent than from high individual marginal rates. Nevertheless, the taxation of excess profits at rates approximating 100 per cent is politically more feasible than severe individual taxation. Efficiency considerations are not the true limiting factors.

Direct controls and the progressiveness of taxation.—The foregoing section argues that reliance on inflationary methods of borrowing, rather than on progressive income taxation, cannot be justified convincingly in terms of incentives. The failure to substitute nonprogressive taxes for inflationary methods could be justified even less by the necessity of maintaining incentives. For linear taxation, marginal rates coincide with average rates, and consequently marginal rates would not reach or approximate 100 per cent before average rates should reach or approximate this level. Even if it were likely that individual marginal tax rates of, say, more than 80 per cent would reduce the quality and quantity of the individual effort, this still would not explain why inflation is not avoided through consumption taxes of sufficient height. On the assumption that high wartime marginal rates, even if confined to the upper brackets and even if alleviated by postwar credits, would reduce efficiency, a case could be established against excessive reliance on progressive income taxes; but the argument could not be used to justify inflation as against taxation in general.

If, however, no adverse effects are expected from high wartime marginal rates, income taxation is more consistent with the direct controls of a war economy than are consumption taxes. The direct controls tend to distribute the war burden on equalitarian principles. The size of rations does not depend on the financial status of the consumer. Financial means would enter into the determination of individual consumption even in an all-inclusive system of rationing, because money is needed to buy the rations. Yet in such a system the relative weight of financial means as determinants of individual consumption would be strongly reduced. Consequently, the controls would render unspendable a larger amount of redundant income in the high-income classes than in the low. Progressive taxes are more nearly the fiscal complements of direct controls than are consumption taxes, because a progressive tax scale, if it reaches down into the low brackets, may be set up in such a manner as to tax away redundant income from the different brackets in approximately that proportion in which the controls render incomes unspendable in the different income classes. The consumption tax, on the other hand, withdraws a higher share of the redundant income accumulated by the low-income classes.

This should not make one forget, however, that uncontrolled or incompletely controlled inflation is much more harmful than the usual types of regressive taxation. An inflationary rise in the price level shares all the disadvantages of regressive taxes and has important additional drawbacks. In terms of efficiency, there exists the significant difference that an inflationary spiral tends to draw away resources from the war segment of the economy into the consumer-goods industries and into purely speculative types of "capital formation," whereas consumption taxes do not give rise to this tendency. So far as the general welfare is affected, the disadvantage of uncontrolled inflation is that it is cumulative and may hit basic necessaries with much greater severity than would consumption taxes.

The basic cause of war inflation.—The conclusion is that the usual methods of war finance cannot be explained on assumptions of rationality. A rational interpretation of the war-finance policies actually applied would be possible only on assumptions which would be clearly unrealistic if applied to the past and which seem no less unrealistic at present. The "rational" case for the typical policies of war finance would have to rest on the following two assumptions: (1) it would have to be assumed that substantially higher individual income taxation than that actually applied would reduce economic efficiency; and (2) it would have to be assumed that total taxation, direct and indirect, typically was sufficient to reduce the inflationary gap to a level at which inflation control would become completely effective and at which postwar disturbances, arising from the inflationary character of war finance, could be avoided. The first of these two assumptions would be necessary to explain why income taxes are not raised beyond the levels actually reached in time of war; and furthermore, it would be necessary to make the second assumption in order to explain why the inflationary gaps of war periods are not reduced below their actual size by means of higher consumption taxes. These assumptions are obviously unrealistic when applied to major wars of the past. The inflation potential generated by major wars typically was too high to be suppressed by direct controls during war periods, and too high, also, to be kept from causing disturbances in postwar periods. The inflation potential generated by the present war is very high, too, not merely in this country, but also in allied and enemy countries alike.

The insufficiency of taxation in war periods is a consequence of political circumstances. The advantage of taxation as rationally viewed is at the same time its main drawback where politics is concerned. Taxation implies a planned distribution of the war burden. Communities do not agree in advance on the distribution of the entire economic burden of a major war. *The inflation potential may be viewed as reflecting the residual on which no explicit agreement has been reached.* The amounts of money corresponding to this residual remain in the ownership of the public. For the duration of the war, direct measures of control such as price control and rationing are intended to prevent the public from using the money corresponding to the residual under consideration. To the extent to which the direct controls enforce the saving of excess incomes they establish a planned distribution of the consumption burden for the duration of the war. Yet when, after the war, the controls are abandoned, one person receives a postwar credit at the expense of the other, in proportion as he was able to store up redundant income during the war. Moreover, to the extent to which the controls fail to prevent the spending of redundant income during the war, the relative burden of different groups is immediately affected by the insufficiency of taxation.

For the community as a whole the inflation potential is clearly harmful. During the war, the community cannot use the excess money to buy more commodities without reducing the efficiency of the war economy; and after the war, the available output flow of commodities and of services will not depend on the stock of money and of claims accumulated during the war period. But, unfortunately, it is not pointless for the individual to accumulate redundant income, because his position is thereby improved in relation to other individuals, who accumulate smaller redundant income or none at all. The individual may ultimately do harm to himself by doing harm to the community. Yet this only means that it would be preferable to agree on the distribution of the entire war burden. After all, the war burden is distributed in some fashion even if inflation is not avoided. A distribution of the war burden in the same fashion by taxation would always be preferable since, in this event, at least the additional burden resulting from the inefficiencies caused by the inflationary process could have been avoided. Moreover, the majority of the population usually feels that it would have been preferable to distribute the burden in some different fashion, because the inflationary process is generally felt to render the distribution of the war burden less equitable. The basic fact, however, is that the "agreement" regarding the specific distribution to be established does not, in reality, extend to the entire war burden. Inflation is the monetary complement of the residual, with respect to which no agreement has been reached.

A brief way of expressing the same notion would be as follows. Part of the war burden is distributed by the inflationary process, controlled or uncontrolled, because the community could not agree in advance to distribute that share of the burden in the manner in which inflation actually turns out to have distributed it, or in any other manner. Consequently, an inflationary residual is created the control of which is costly and, especially if the postwar period is included, necessarily incomplete.

In reality, such widely different war economies as those of the United States, Great Britain, Germany, Italy, and Japan have in common a reliance on the method of controlled inflation. Although differences in degree should not be overlooked, nevertheless in the mature stage of the war effort taxation yields, or in all probability will yield, less than one-half the annual war fund required by each country[6] and a large portion of the borrowing is from banks. Each country has an elaborate system of direct controls aiming at the suppression of the inflation potential generated by its war finance. According to present American plans, taxation will contribute about 30 billions to the requirements of the Treasury during the fiscal year ending with June, 1943. About 45 billions would have to be raised by borrowing and a considerable share of the borrowing would undoubtedly have to be in the form of security sales to banks. The general price ceiling order, issued on April 28, 1942, and the rationing of consumers' goods are intended to keep the public from spending redundant income during the war. These measures, in conjunction with priorities and with the allocation of resources, aim at suppressing such expenditures as would impair the efficiency of the war sector or the equitable distribution of the war burden. Much the greater part of the spending potential to be suppressed is being simultaneously created by the methods of war finance.

---

[6] With respect to Canada see, however, Postscript on Recent Developments, pp. 148 ff.

However, a comparison of World War I with the present war seems to indicate a world trend toward increased reliance on taxation. The inflation potential caused by the "residual" previously discussed is high in the present war; but it is typically lower *relative to the annual war fund* than it was in World War I. The specific agreement concerning the distribution of the war burden now relates to a higher share of the total burden, and the controls seem to be both more inclusive and more systematically enforced throughout the world. In relation to significant economic magnitudes, the inflation potential may of course turn out to be no smaller, or even to be greater, than in the last war. The present war is more costly in relation to significant economic magnitudes—such as, for example, total output—than was the war of 1914–1918.

The effectiveness of inflation control.—Effectiveness and ineffectiveness of inflation control are not clear-cut concepts. There are different types of effectiveness which should be distinguished from one another, as will be discussed later in some detail. The controls may, by preventing the expenditure of redundant incomes, induce the public to buy government securities; they may, by preventing the expenditure of redundant incomes, induce the public to accumulate idle cash; or they may, by preventing the expenditure of redundant incomes on certain goods, induce the public to increase its expenditures on less essential commodities.[7] The controls are ineffective to the extent that they do not possess effectiveness in any of these senses. Ineffectiveness need not reflect itself fully in the existence of bootleg markets. It may reflect itself partly in the necessity of raising ceiling prices in order to avoid bootleg markets; also, in the inability of the legislative or of the executive authority to resist political influences aiming at discrimi-

---

[7] On commodities or services which are not considered basic necessities and which, at the same time, do not compete directly with war materials on the supply side. This, however, is a matter of degree. The "Kalecki plan" would ration the sum total of individual consumer expenditure in addition to rationing certain commodities specifically.

natory treatment in favor of certain strategic prices. This last point is all the more worth emphasizing because in this country wage rates and certain agricultural commodities[8] are thus far exempt from the ceiling order.[9] It will be suggested (in chapter vi) that the deterioration of the quality of commodities at unchanging prices is an essentially "inflationary" phenomenon reflecting the ineffectiveness of controls only if a unit of physical factor input yields a greater quantity of the inferior product than of the original commodity. If the output–input ratio is not higher for the inferior product than previously for the original commodity, then the deterioration of quality at unchanging prices is more a consumption tax than an "inflationary" phenomenon because the money earnings (per unit of factor input) obtainable through the production of the commodity in question do not then increase.[10]

Of the various types of effectiveness, that which induces the public to buy government securities is the most desirable. The controls perform their function better if they induce the public to save and to buy government securities (or to repay bank loans) than if they induce saving and the hoarding of cash. To the extent to which redundant incomes flow back into the market for government securities, it is not necessary to continue borrowing operations from the banks.[11] If all redundant incomes were to flow back against war bonds, the first installment of the new money borrowed from banks could finance a constant rate of deficit spending for an indefinite time, and a small

---

[8] Mostly those products the prices of which at the farm have not yet reached 110 per cent of parity.

[9] If wage rates could be stabilized *de facto* without the formal placing of a ceiling on them, such a procedure, as an act of liberal policy, might have certain advantages. It is very unlikely, however, that this could be accomplished, especially should entrepreneurs continue to be free to compete for scarce labor. After having bid up their costs, they have a "just claim" for revision of the ceiling prices of their products. Moreover, under "cost-plus contracts" with the government, the revision is automatic. The ceiling order does not apply to armament products purchased by the government.

[10] Cf. the definition of inflation in fn. 1, p. 2.

[11] To the extent to which bank loans are repaid the additional borrowing from banks is offset by the repayments.

additional amount of money would have to be borrowed from the banks only when the current rate of deficit spending should increase. If, however, the controls, by rendering redundant incomes unspendable, merely induce the public to accumulate idle cash, then the government must go on borrowing from banks and increasing the stock of money at a substantial rate. These money hoards endanger the effectiveness of the controls during the war and are apt to "explode" at the wrong moment after the war. Lending of redundant incomes to the government removes the menace for the duration of the war, assuming that the owners of government securities cannot claim redemption during the war, or that they may be trusted not to do so; and it diminishes the inflation potential of the postwar period, because redemption is likely to extend over a rather long time. Nevertheless, controlled inflation leaves a transfer problem to the postwar world even to the extent to which the money is lent back to the government, and in this respect it compares unfavorably with taxation regardless of the type of effectiveness which may be expected from the controls.

The type and the degree of effectiveness to be expected depend, of course, largely on the monetary pressure which the controls have to overcome. The smaller the pressure, the easier it is to prevent harmful spending during the war and the better are the chances that the controls may be liquidated without substantial inflationary consequences after the war. A small amount of redundant income is also more likely to be conducted into the market of government securities than a substantial amount. A high inflation potential, even if successfully suppressed for the duration of the war, is likely to result in the large-scale accumulation of idle balances. Both type and degree of effectiveness become less satisfactory as the pressure rises.

The monetary pressure against which the controls operate may be said to depend on the amount of savings which would genuinely tend to be forthcoming in the given circumstances, even in the absence of consumer controls. Either the excess of the deficit over genuine savings[12] will be transformed into induced savings by the working of the controls, or it will result in inflationary developments. The magnitude of the pressure is measured by that amount of additional saving[13] which the controls would have to enforce in order to prevent the inflationary process.

It is impossible to estimate the "genuine tendency to save" on reliable grounds. A tentative estimate (given in chapter vi) would indicate that in the circumstances to be expected for the fiscal year 1942-43, genuine savings out of American gross money income[14] would not exceed 20 billions. Considering that the deficit is expected to reach a level of about 45 billions, this means that the controls, in order to be completely effective, would have to enforce an exceedingly high amount of additional saving. Regardless of the reliability of estimates like this, it is obvious that the American system of controls will have to overcome a very substantial monetary pressure unless taxation is increased well beyond the level now contemplated. The controls of the other countries also operate against a rather large inflation potential. Although it is difficult to appraise the significance of violations and of other forms of ineffectiveness in these countries, there are strong indications that a substantial portion of savings enforced by the controls fails to flow back to the market of government securities.

Summary.—Social communities are unwilling or unable to agree in advance upon the specific distribution of the entire burden imposed upon them by major wars; hence, inflationary war finance. To the extent to which direct controls are effective during the war—and they are never completely effective—an

---

[12] More precisely: the excess of the deficit over such genuine gross savings as are not offset by private gross investment expenditures. Private net investment may be assumed to become negative, since capital consumption will presumably outweigh the relatively small amount of private war investment.

[13] Additional as compared with the "genuine" savings which would accrue even in the absence of consumer controls.

[14] More precisely: the excess of genuine gross savings over maintenance expenditures plus privately financed war investment.

agreement is implicitly reached for the duration; but, since the frozen portion of the redundant incomes becomes purchasing power in the postwar period, the public acquires a postwar credit. In terms of real goods this postwar credit is entirely meaningless for the public as a whole, but it affects the distribution of real goods between the various sections of the population because different income recipients are left with different amounts of frozen income.

If the inflationary residual becomes high, the effectiveness of the controls is likely to be reduced during the war and genuine inflationary developments to become unavoidable in the postwar period. Uncontrolled or incompletely controlled war inflation, by stimulating the diversion of resources into the civilian segment of the economy, constitutes a serious menace to armament production. Moreover, both war and postwar inflation render the distribution of real incomes highly inequitable. Increased reliance on taxation should emphatically be welcomed, because it reflects the extension of the agreement—of the social contract, as it were—to a higher share of the war burden. Everybody has a preference for some specific agreement: for some specific tax structure, or some specific combination of taxation with compulsory lending. But in war finance almost any agreement is preferable to lack of agreement. Indeed, it would be hard to invent a tax which would be as harmful as an inflationary gap of unmanageable size.

CHAPTER II

The Stimulus to Civilian Production in the Period of Nonbelligerency

● *Induced consumption and induced investment.*—Following the outbreak in Europe of the present world war, there was a growing awareness in this country that the Axis powers would sooner or later attack the United States. In consequence, the economy of the United States gradually came to differ only in degree from a wartime economy. The difference in degree was substantial, however. After the fall of France in June, 1940, the defense program, in the technical sense, was adopted. Yet, when the Japanese attacked Pearl Harbor in December, 1941, the American economy still was primarily a consumption economy rather than a defense economy even though the significance of the defense sector was growing.

The rapidly rising rate of defense spending is shown by table 1. Aggregate defense expenditures of the federal government and of the Reconstruction Finance Corporation from June, 1940, to the end of 1941 exceeded 15 billions. Part of these expenditures should be regarded as investment outlays rather than as running costs of the defense machinery. Expenditures on existing assets rather than on current output are also included.

It would be misleading to regard the resources acquired for these defense outlays as a measure of the real burden of defense during the period under consideration. This would imply that the resources used for defense would otherwise have been utilized in the production of goods for civilian use (which hereafter will be referred to more briefly as "civilian output"). Such an assumption would probably be quite unrealistic since a sub-

Stimulus to Civilian Production

stantial part of the American resources had not been utilized since the great depression.

If we attempt to calculate the burden by comparing the output of 1939 with the civilian output of later years, then the

TABLE 1
UNITED STATES WAR EXPENDITURES—JULY, 1940–DECEMBER, 1941
(In millions of dollars)

Date	Expenditures[a]	Change from preceding month
1940		
July	186	....
August	213	+ 27
September	234	+ 21
October	312	+ 78
November	391	+ 79
December	483	+ 92
1941		
January	589	+ 106
February	607	+ 18
March	797	+ 190
April	824	+ 27
May	904	+ 80
June	890	− 14
July	1,021	+ 131
August	1,190	+ 169
September	1,424	+ 234
October	1,658	+ 234
November	1,532	− 126
December	1,997[b]	+ 465[b]
Total	15,252	....

[a] Checks paid by the United States Treasury and the Reconstruction Finance Corporation, for war purposes.
[b] Preliminary figures.
SOURCE: *Victory*, January 13, 1942, p. 32.

burden appears to be negative for the period. The civilian output of the years 1940 and 1941 was considerably greater than that of 1939. This method of calculating the "burden," however, also rests on assumptions of doubtful validity. Nevertheless, it is interesting to compare the civilian output of war years with that of a base period—for which 1939 may be chosen. The question of whether it is meaningful to derive the magnitude of the defense burden, or of the net gain attributable to defense, from such a comparison will be discussed later.

It should be pointed out that the American output flow of the base year 1939 was higher than the output of any other year during the 1930's. The base year of the present-day war economy is one of relatively high output in terms of post depression conditions. By calling 1939 a year of high output merely in relation to postdepression years I do not mean to imply that the output flow of 1939 was lower absolutely than that of the late 1920's. On the contrary, 1929 was the only year in which the level of 1939 (and the approximately equal level of 1937) had previously been reached.[1] But the fact that the 1929 level was not exceeded in the subsequent decade by any considerable margin proves the absence of an upward trend in the 1930's. If we assume that an upward trend is "normal," then the output flow of 1939 must be regarded as relatively low. If, however, we take the stagnant trend of the 1930's as

[1] The industrial production index of the Federal Reserve Board is 110 for 1929, 113 for 1937, and 108 for 1939 (1935–1939 = 100).

The Department of Commerce estimates of income produced in current prices are 83.3 billions for 1929, 71.5 billions for 1937, and 70.8 billions for 1939. The Department has also corrected these figures for price changes. The difference between the corrected data relating to three years is small. The corrected figure for 1939 is slightly higher than that for 1937, and the figure for 1937 is slightly higher than that for 1929. Professor Kuznets' figures in *National Income and Its Composition, 1919–1938* would indicate that national income in 1929 prices was more in 1929 than in 1937, but 1929 is the only year of the 'twenties for which this is true.

The income estimates here referred to relate to national income at factor costs, i.e., to the aggregate earnings of the factors of production. It will be argued in the next chapter that changes in the national income at (constant) market prices provide better measures for changes in net output in the here relevant sense. The conclusion concerning the relative size of output in 1929, 1937, and 1939 would not be changed, however, if the figures were corrected for the difference existing between national income at factor costs and national income at market prices. The difference, as will be seen, consists of the taxes paid by or through business firms. According to recent estimates, these tax yields amounted to 7 billions in 1929, 9 billions in 1937, and 9.6 billions in 1939 (see *Survey of Current Business*, May, 1942, p. 12).

Stimulus to Civilian Production 25

the basis for reference, then the year of the outbreak of the war in Europe appears as a year of high business activity.

In 1940 and 1941 it was possible to expand the output of the American economy far beyond its prewar level. The rise in real output was greater than the rise in armament production. Consequently, if the burden of the defense effort is calculated simply by comparing the prewar civilian output with that of the subsequent years, there appears to be a net gain, rather than a burden. In Keynesian terminology this would be expressed by saying that the expenditures occasioned by the war gave rise to a Multiplier Effect and that, in addition to this, the marginal efficiency of capital increased. As a consequence of increased consumption and of increased nondefense investment the rise in aggregate real output was in excess of the rise directly occasioned by the war.

The rise of real consumption from 1939 to 1940 was small, but the rise from 1939 to 1941 was substantial. The value of the additional real consumption flow during this two-year period may have been on the order of 12 billions in 1939 prices.[2] The value of the entire additional net output flow during the period was on the order of 30 to 35 billions, as expressed in the prices of the same year.[3] It follows that almost 40 per cent of the addi-

---

[2] In 1939, consumers' purchases amounted to 61 billions, in 1940 to 65 billions, and in 1941 to 74 billions in current prices. The price change between 1939 and 1940 is negligible; the 1941 figure, however, should be deflated by about 6 per cent, the cost of living correction. Consequently, the increment in "real" consumption beyond the 1939 level was 4 billions in 1940 and 8 to 9 billions in 1941. The cumulative difference is around 12 billions. (See Milton Gilbert, "War Expenditures and National Production," *Survey of Current Business*, March, 1942, table 2, on p. 11. Somewhat earlier estimates published by the O.P.M. lead to the same conclusion; see Grace W. Knott, *Estimated Distribution of Civilian Expenditures, 1940, 1941, and 1942*.)

[3] National income at market prices amounted to 80.4 billions in 1933, 89.1 billions in 1940, and 112.3 billions in 1941. If the price change between 1939 and 1940 is disregarded and the 1941 figure is deflated by about 6 per cent, then the additional real output in excess of the 1939 level is found to be 8.7 billions in 1940 and about 25 billions in 1941. The cumulative difference is then around 33 to 34 billions. Figures used here relate to national income at market prices rather than to national income at factor costs because they are a better expression of changes in the flow of net output. This point will be discussed in the following chapter; pp. 41–42.

tional output, as compared with the 1939 level, may have gone into consumption. The greater proportion was taken up partly by the defense activities of the government and partly by increased private capital formation, including additions to inventories. Some of the private capital formation also served the purpose of the defense program; but if we assume that only half the increase in capital formation was for nondefense purposes, then the share of the rise in real output absorbed by the civilian sector would already reach 50 per cent.[4]

By 1941 the flow of real consumption seems to have risen to a level exceeding that of 1939 by roughly 15 per cent. We are used to regarding a rise of this magnitude as a "substantial" rise. For example, during the great depression the decline in total real consumption was on the order of 25 per cent and the subsequent rise during the recovery seems to have exceeded 30 per cent by a slight margin. The rise which occurred from 1939 to 1941 was well over half as great as was the shrinkage which had occurred during the great depression, and about half as great as the subsequent rise to the peak level of the 'thirties. Statements like these may, of course, be misleading in several ways since the significance of changes in consumption cannot be appraised without analyzing the breakdown of total consumption into various constituents, and likewise the distribution of consumption among different sections of the population. To derive "real" magnitudes for the economy as a whole by correcting aggregate value figures for price changes is a highly formalistic procedure which at best can only serve the purpose of illustrating rough orders of magnitude. The figures resulting from the foregoing calculations must not be interpreted in any other way. They illustrate that much of the additional output flow went into consumption and that the percentage rise in real consumption was large. It should be

---

[4] Private gross capital expenditures were in excess of their 1939 level by 3.1 billions in 1940 and by 6.2 billions in 1941. The cumulative difference, as compared with the 1939 level, amounts to 9.3 billions. A slight downward correction is appropriate, however, for price changes and for increased maintenance (see Milton Gilbert, *loc. cit.*).

Stimulus to Civilian Production

added that the proportionate rise in the flow of durable consumers' goods was much in excess of the average rise in aggregate consumption. According to Dr. Terborgh's and Dr. Dirks's estimates, the expenditures of final buyers on these goods rose 18 per cent between 1939 and 1940 and 44 per cent between 1939 and 1941. The rise in other consumers' expeditures was

TABLE 2
ESTIMATED EXPENDITURES FOR NEW CONSUMERS' EQUIPMENT[a]

	Expenditures (In millions of dollars)			Percentage increases (In current prices)		
	1939	1940	1941	1939–1940	1940–1941	1939–1941
Consumers' equipment..........	6,980	8,250	10,060	18.2	21.9	44.1
Passenger cars.....	2,230	2,950	3,490	32.3	18.3	56.5
Household goods...	4,750	5,300	6,570	11.6	24.0	38.3

[a] From George Terborgh, "Durable Goods Expenditures in 1940," *Federal Reserve Bulletin*, February, 1941, p. 103; Frederick C. Dirks, "Durable Goods Expenditures in 1941," *Federal Reserve Bulletin*, April, 1942, p. 317.

distinctly smaller. Recent estimates put it at 6 per cent and 17 per cent, respectively.[5] These estimates run in current prices.

Such developments were of course a consequence of the fact that in 1939 the resources of the American economy were incompletely utilized. Without the existence of unutilized productive capacities and of unemployed labor reserves, defense production would necessarily have been associated with a reduction of civilian output. It is interesting to note in this connection that the ratio of aggregate real capital to aggregate real output does not seem to have changed significantly from 1929 to 1939. In spite of this, it is likely that excess capacities were much greater at the outbreak of the war in Europe than ten years earlier.

[5] The Terborgh method does not distinguish between final buyers who are consumers and final buyers who are producers. However, Dr. Gilbert's estimates in the March issue of the *Survey of Current Business* lead to the conclusion that the percentage rise in consumer outlay on the commodities in question was almost precisely the same. The Terborgh-Dirks figures are used here because they are broken down by types of durable goods.

The assumption that the capital-output ratio did not change markedly in the decade following 1929 is based on two facts. The real output flow of 1939 was not very different in magnitude from the real output flow of 1929.[6] At the same time, the new capital formation of the period 1930–1938 cannot have increased the aggregate stock of real capital in any high proportion. Up to 1937 the net investment of the recovery was but a flow of deferred replacements, if the economy is viewed as one unit.[7] It took more than the capital formation of the years 1935 and 1936 to offset the net capital consumption of the period 1930–1934. The net real investment of the entire eight-year period was less than the growth of the capital stock in any one of the high years during the 1920's; and the investment of 1937 consisted to a relatively large extent of an increase in business inventories rather than of plant expansion. In the aggregate there was not much more real capital in the American economy in 1939 than in 1929.[8] Hence it may be assumed that the capital-output ratio was also roughly the same in 1939 as ten years earlier. Nevertheless, it is clear that the unutilized share of resources was high at the outbreak of the war in Europe.

The existence of unutilized industrial capacities and of unemployed labor resources rendered it possible to expand industrial production at more or less stable prices up to February, 1941. In the eighteen-month period lying between the outbreak of the war and February, 1941, the general level of wholesale prices rose only by about 7 per cent.[9] By that time, industrial production exceeded its prewar level by about 35

---

[6] See footnote 1, p. 24.

[7] According to Professor Kuznets' estimates, the total net capital formation of the period 1930–1938 amounted to only 6.1 billions in 1929 prices. Simon Kuznets, *National Income and Its Composition*, National Bureau of Economic Research, 1941.

[8] The reader should, of course, be reminded of the qualifications to which statements like this are subject owing to the change in the composition of the real capital stock.

[9] The U. S. Department of Labor wholesale price index was 75.0 for August, 1939, and 80.6 for February, 1941.

Stimulus to Civilian Production

per cent, and nonagricultural employment was in excess of its 1939 level by almost 4 million persons.[10] After February, 1941, the rise in wholesale prices and the rate of increase in the hitherto stable cost of living became marked. For a few months both industrial output and the price level were rising rapidly. Since June, 1941, the rise in aggregate industrial production has slowed down substantially, yet prices have continued to rise.

There is a strong presumption that the excess capacities were largely concentrated in the durable goods industries. We have said above that in 1939 the real output flow of the economy as well as the real capital stock were approximately at their 1929 levels. Industrial production, that is, manufacturing plus mining, which in 1939 accounted for about 25 per cent of all output,[11] was also at the same level in 1939 as prior to the great depression. But within the aggregate of industrial production the relative share of durable manufactures had declined significantly and that of the nondurable industries had, of course, risen correspondingly.[12] This is a reflection of the fact that in 1939, as compared with the late 1920's, investment flowing into residential housing and into plant and equipment accounted for only a small share of the total output. Moreover, the share of the flow of durable consumers' goods had also declined.[13] Consequently, the durable-goods industries were producing at a rate falling far short of the rate of production they had reached in the preceding decade. The opposite was true of the nondurable-goods industries; their output was considerably in

[10] See tables 1 and 2 in the Appendix.
[11] For the composition of aggregate output see table 3 in Appendix.
[12] Federal Reserve Board Index (1935–1939 = 100)

	1929	1939
Total industrial production	110	108
Manufactures:		
Durable	132	109
Nondurable	93	108

[13] See table 4 in the Appendix.

excess of previously reached levels. This creates a presumption that the capacities of durable-goods industries were the less utilized. Indeed, during the period of relatively stable prices, that is, up to early in 1941, the expansion of the durable-goods industries was substantially greater,[14] while prices of durable manufactures were more stable. Those few finished product prices which did show a noteworthy rise in the period of relatively stable prices belong for the most part in the nondurable category.

The substantial amount of unemployment, which was another prerequisite of rapid industrial expansion, reflects the circumstance that the increase in output per man-hour plus the population growth had outweighed the shortening of the working week. Census data lead to the conclusion that in 1939 the unemployed portion of what was then considered the "labor force" may have amounted to 7 to 8 million persons.[15] This figure is far in excess of any reasonable estimate for 1929.[16] From 1939 to the end of 1941, nonagricultural employment rose by about 6 million persons (to almost 41 million).[17] The number of nonagricultural man-hours applied in the economy rose in a higher proportion than the corresponding employment figure, since the working week was lengthened. As a consequence, the rise in aggregate labor hours performed amounts to roughly 45 per cent in industries other than agriculture.[18]

These conditions made it possible to add, as it were, a defense section to the normal peacetime economy of the nation

---

[14] The Federal Reserve Board index for durable manufactures rose by 62.3 per cent from August, 1939, to February, 1941. The index for nondurable manufactures rose by 12.2 per cent during the same period.

[15] Preliminary census returns for the period March 24–30, 1940, show that there were 52.841 million persons fourteen years of age and over in the labor force, and that 45.350 million were employed, public emergency workers excepted. The difference between these two figures is 7.491 million unemployed persons: 5.110 million reported as seeking work, and 2.380 million doing public emergency work.

[16] See Russell A. Nixon and Paul A. Samuelson, "Estimates of Unemployment in the United States," *Review of Economic Statistics*, August, 1940.

[17] See table 2 in the Appendix.

[18] See table 5 in the Appendix.

without reducing the output flow of the "normal" sector. On the contrary, the stimulus derived from building up the defense section was allowed to have its effects on business activity within the peacetime sector. As we have seen, up to the end of 1941 one-half (or less) of the slack existing at the outbreak of the war was taken up by defense activities. Owing to the rise in the rate of human consumption and to the increase in private capital formation, about one-half (possibly more) of the unutilized resources was used to expand nondefense production.

The real burden of the armament program was negative during the first two years, if the real burden is calculated this way. Competent economists as well as laymen believed that the policies which led to the Multiplier Effect in question were clearly justified and that a flow of consumption exceeding the prewar level might well become stabilized for the duration of the war. It is now common knowledge that civilian consumption will have to be substantially curtailed. As a matter of fact, it was obvious before the attack on Pearl Harbor that the continued increase in armament production had to become associated with a decline in output for civilion needs. Published figures relating to the war-production program now provide a rough basis on which to estimate the necessary degree of curtailment, and we must conclude that consumption of both durable and nondurable items will have to be reduced below prewar levels. Prior to Pearl Harbor a basis was lacking because the plans relating to the aggregate of armament production and to its time rate were changing at frequent intervals. The planned figures were rising all the time, but no official estimate was given of the probable time rate of defense spending in future fiscal years, and the aggregate appropriations, which are rather meaningless so long as the time rate remains indeterminate, were obviously not final. In spite of this, it was well known before the summer of 1941 that a drastic reduction in the production of durable consumer goods would become indispensable; in fact, the defense agencies started to curtail the output of the durable consumer goods industries several months before the close of the period of nonbelligerency.

The period in which practically all industries were expanding came to an end in the summer of 1941. The upward movement in aggregate industrial production had to overcome

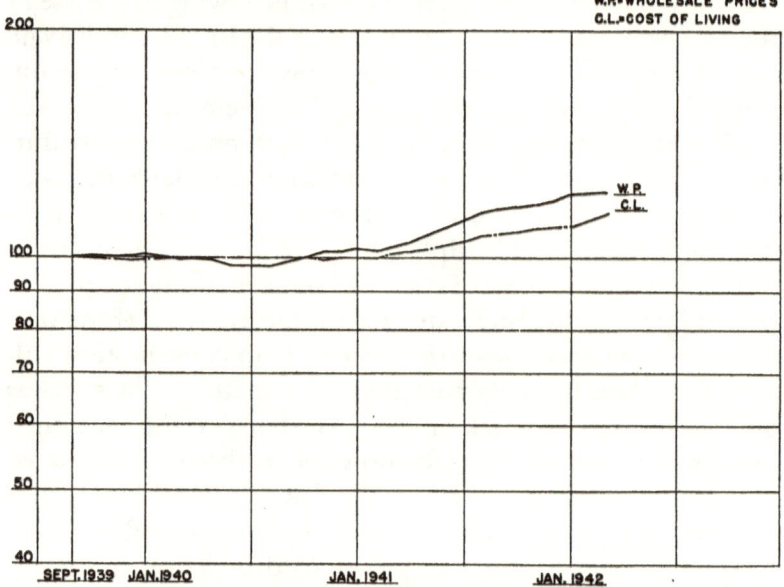

Chart 1. Wholesale prices and the cost of living. Converted to September, 1939 = 100.

increasing obstacles, as already was clearly to be seen in data available prior to the summer months. A marked upward trend in both the wholesale price index and the cost of living became apparent in the spring months.

Average hourly earnings of labor also rose at an accelerated rate after the spring months of 1941, but, owing to the rise in the cost of living, the increase in "real" hourly earnings almost entirely ceased. This may be interpreted to reflect the diminution of the available slack. The actual shrinkage in the civilian sector did not, however, show up before June, 1941, after which the rise in armament production took place largely at the ex-

Stimulus to Civilian Production

pense of other items of output.[19] Since that time, aggregate industrial production has risen but slightly. The total rise in the seasonally adjusted index amounts to about 5 per cent for the second half of 1941, whereas it amounted to 14 per cent for the first half of the year and to more than 30 per cent

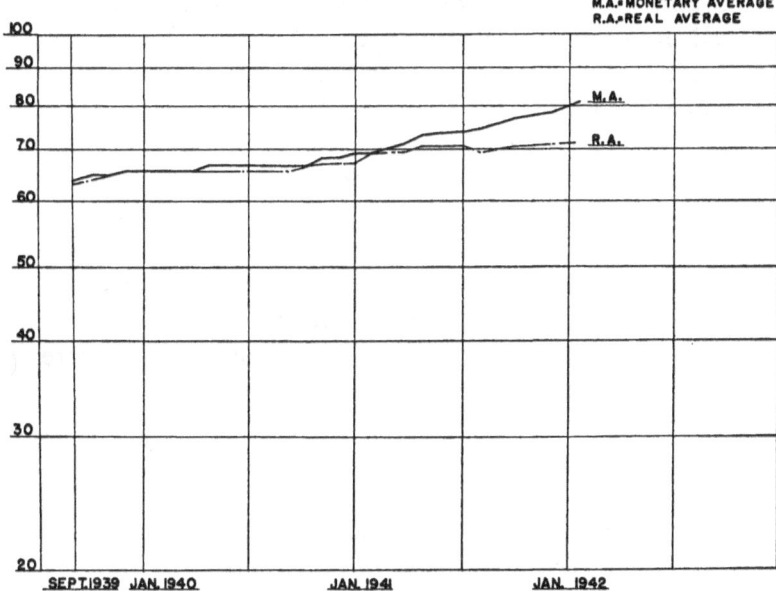

Chart 2. Monetary and real average hourly earnings.

for the twelve-month period between the summer of 1940 and the summer of 1941. The extent of the future curtailment likely to occur in the civilian sector will be discussed in the next chapter.

The question now arises whether it is not misleading to view the increased civilian output of the first two years as a "negative burden" or "net gain" when it is obvious that the temporarily increased output flow of the civilian sector will have to be curtailed. One is, of course, free to define the real burden in such a way that the rise in civilian output appears to

[19] See table 7 in the Appendix.

be a "net gain." Is it, however, reasonable to define it thus without qualifications? The answer, I believe, is no.

If we confine ourselves to a comparison of the years 1940 and 1941 with some prewar year, we do not merely choose an arbitrary base period; we at the same time disregard a number of important causal relationships between past and future, as viewed from the present juncture. The choice of an arbitrary base year is unavoidable, but there is no need to overlook important relationships between past and future developments.

Past "gain" and future effort.—The burden of reaching the 1941 armament output cannot be viewed independently of the burden to be imposed on the public in the future course of the war. The sacrifice to be borne in the future has undoubtedly been increased because at the beginning the resources of the economy were incompletely mobilized for the defense effort. Moreover, it must be assumed that the increase of the future burden occasioned by the "gain" of the first two years outweighs this gain. If it were reasonable to assume that "one unit" of past gain would give rise to merely one unit of additional future burden, there would be no objection to deriving the total burden of the war from the past gain plus the future burden. Yet in reality it is not reasonable to assume that the burden has merely been postponed. It has been postponed and increased. Now it is obviously misleading not to debit an economic process with a cost to which the process itself gives rise in future periods.

One might argue, in terms of utility theory, that an uneven time distribution of a consumption burden always tends to increase the sacrifice beyond the necessary level. The argument would have to hold that it is a smaller sacrifice to curtail the rate of consumption from level A to level B for the duration of a war than first to increase the rate of consumption beyond A and then to curtail it to a level falling short of B. Such reasoning based on the assumption of diminishing marginal utility does contain an element of truth, but it is difficult to

Stimulus to Civilian Production

evaluate its significance. Subjective value theorizing over time is always precarious, and it becomes especially so if the psychology of a community undergoes a radical change within the period over which the analysis is extended. A smaller burden may be felt more painfully by a "nonbelligerent" community than a greater burden by a community involved in an actual "shooting war." Hence the psychological aspects of the problem are not those which I should like to emphasize in the present context.

By saying that the burden was not merely postponed, but that at the same time it was increased, I mean something more specific: more resources must now be diverted to the war effort because they were not diverted earlier. The rate of expansion in the defense industries could have been substantially greater if some burden had been imposed upon the public from the outset. If merely the additional consumption flow of 1940 and 1941 (over 1939) had been diverted, this would have changed substantially the rate of expansion in the defense industries. The value of the additional consumption flow during the two years under consideration[20] was about 17 billions in current prices. If the nondefense investment of the two years be added to this, a sum of more than 20 billions may result.[21] As against this the value of all approved defense-plant expansion, including new equipment, was slightly more than 7 billions through December, 1941.[22] All defense investments since the outbreak of the war in Europe may have amounted to somewhat more than this. The working capital corresponding to the defense-plant expansion would have to be taken into account, and it would be necessary to add the investment in defense industries prior to the start of the "defense program" in the official sense. A downward correction is called for, on the other hand, by

---

[20] "Additional" in the sense of "in excess of the 1939 level."

[21] The "additional" private capital expenditures during the two years were estimated at 9.3 billions. This figure includes, however, some private defense investment and also some increase in maintenance expenditures.

[22] See *Victory*, March 17, 1942, p. 16.

the fact that not all the defense investment projects approved through December, 1941, were actually carried out by this date. The appropriate upward corrections may perhaps amount to somewhat more than the downward correction, although not necessarily so. At any rate, it is obvious that the speed with which resources were mobilized for the defense effort could have been increased in a very high proportion had the "stimulus" on the civilian segment of the economy been suppressed and had the defense effort been correspondingly increased. This is true even if account is taken of the fact that an increased rate of mobilization would have been associated with increased frictions and consequently with an increased temporary waste in the form of "priorities" unemployment.

Had the "gain" under consideration been suppressed and the defense effort correspondingly increased, then one of two things would have happened. A given stage of preparedness as measured in terms of war-material producing capacities might have been reached at an earlier date. This probably would have reduced the aggregate effort, as expressed in terms of war equipment and labor hours, required to attain the objectives of the present war. Or, alternatively, if the time rate of future war-material production had not been affected by the early mobilization of resources, fewer resources would have been diverted from their civilian uses in the future course of the war—fewer not merely by the amount of those resources which would have been diverted in the past, but fewer by more than this amount. To make the point specific: the sooner resources are diverted to the production of airplane-manufacturing equipment, the fewer will be the resources required to produce airplane-manufacturing capacities of given size by, say, the end of 1943. A large amount of resources is required to build up war-material producing plants of a given size quickly: a smaller amount will suffice if the plants are built up over a longer period. The same, of course, is true of the immediate war materials themselves (i.e., of airplanes rather than of airplane-manufacturing capacities). Yet, since stages of preparedness are better measured in terms of war-material producing capacities than in terms of war-material inventories, it seems preferable to stress plant capacities.

Whatever plants (or ultimate war materials) we designate as appropriate measures of the economic war potential, the specialized productive capacities necessary to construct the required number of plants, or to produce the required quantity of war materials, within one year will always be more than the specialized productive capacities necessary to construct the required number of plants, or to produce the required quantity of war materials, within two years. Consequently, postponed mobilization is not simply a matter of increasing the later war input by the amount by which it failed to be increased at an earlier stage. Postponed mobilization does not merely mean that the same specialized capacities have to be constructed in less time; it means that greater capacities have to be built because the same capacities will not produce the same output in less time. If new plants constitute the "output" under consideration, this is just as true as when we have an output of final commodities in mind.

The problem we are considering is one of complementarity over time. One can so refine the concept of the real burden as to allow for this phenomenon, but if it is thus refined it loses its determinateness completely. The real burden, defined as foregone civilian output of a specific period, becomes a determinate magnitude on the arbitrary assumption that the output of some base year provides an acceptable zero level. All the logical deficiencies of deriving real magnitudes by correcting money values for price changes are, of course, inherent in this "determinate" concept.[23] But the concept shares these deficiencies with all magnitudes designated as real. As against this, we must abandon all appearance of quantitative determinate-

---

[23] The arbitrariness of the line of distinction between defense investment and nondefense investment enters as a further difficulty.

ness if we try to include in our analysis the effects of past processes on future developments, although if we disregard them we get a misleading impression of the problem.

In broad terms and with no attempt at quantitative evaluation, we may, of course, try to appraise these relationships over time and thereby indicate in what direction the outcome of an analysis would have to be corrected for these relationships. We have seen, for example, that the apparent gain realized during the period of nonbelligerency will give rise to an additional subsequent burden which must be expected to outweigh the gain. This item of correction cannot be appraised quantitatively, but it should not be overlooked. The effect of the increase in the public debt is another matter which cannot be dealt with in quantitative terms but which nevertheless must not be disregarded.

An evaluation of the war burden which would disregard the effects of the public debt on postwar developments would be incomplete in spite of the fact that it is impossible to appraise the magnitude of these effects. It has frequently been pointed out that the interest on an internally held public debt is a "mere" transfer payment. The interest is paid by certain members of the community to other members of the same community. It is incorrect in this sense to say that the people of today, by running into debt, leave a burden to the people of tomorrow. A well-known and neat form of expressing this notion is to say that the people of tomorrow will not merely pay the interest but will also hold the government securities. In spite of this there is a strong presumption that the economic activities of "tomorrow" will be unfavorably affected by a large public debt.

It is possible of course to devise, on paper, a tax system which would eliminate these difficulties. If, for example, every owner of government securities should have to pay additional taxes corresponding precisely to the yield of his securities, there would be no problem. But it is obvious that no real tax sys-

Stimulus to Civilian Production 39

tem operates this way. Consequently, a substantial public debt must be expected to create claims against certain sections of the population in favor of other sections. This, of course, is true of private securities too, although here the individual or the group paying the interest typically acquires, by virtue of running into debt, an additional income stream out of which the obligation can be met. The interest stream on private securities transfers a portion of the earnings of capital to the lenders of capital. Now the interest on the public debt, if met by taxation, transfers further portions of the earnings of capital as well as portions of the earnings of labor to the lenders of such funds as have been used up outside of the contemporary economic processes. It is likely that large transfers of this kind have an unfavorable effect not merely on income distribution but also on the aggregate level of output and of employment. The net reward of enterprise is diminished by high taxes in the event of a favorable outcome; at the same time the loss arising from an unfavorable outcome remains unchanged. The burdening of income-generating activities in favor of the owners of government securities is likely to impair production if interest payments on the public debt become substantial.

We have considered the difficulties arising from a substantial public debt here even though the main increase will be subsequent to the period we are concerned with in the present chapter. Up to the end of the period of nonbelligerency the rise in the interest-bearing public debt amounted to about 15 billions, which is much less than the rise in a single future fiscal year will be.[24] The downward trend of long-term rates continued until Pearl Harbor.[25] The problem was mentioned in the present context merely for the reason that it throws light on the

---

[24] The interest-bearing government debt, other than that held by federal agencies and trust funds, amounted to 39.4 billions in June, 1939, and to 54.3 billions in December, 1941. Securities fully guaranteed by the federal government are included.

[25] Since Pearl Harbor there has been a slight increase in long-term rates. Short-term rates, mainly those on government bills, had already begun to recover slightly in the course of 1941.

inadequacy of all calculations relating to the size of the economic war burden for whatever period the burden may be calculated. As we have seen, the main difficulties arise because past developments are functionally related to future developments. The public debt provides one of the channels through which these effects operate. Here again we must refrain from quantitative appraisal, but we may say something about the direction, that is, the "algebraic sign," of the influence. The effect is an unfavorable one. The past should be debited, rather than credited, for both of the phenomena we have considered.

The conclusion may be expressed in a few sentences stressing different aspects of the situation. The defense expenditures of the federal government plus the defense investment outlays financed by government agencies amounted to about 15 billions during the period under consideration. To call the resources acquired for this amount the real armament burden of the period would imply that the resources in question would otherwise have been utilized for civilian production. There is no reason to assume this. If instead we assume that in the absence of a war economic activities would have continued at their 1939 level, and if at the same time we disregard the complementarity existing between past and future developments, then we might conclude that prior to Pearl Harbor the war gave rise to a substantial economic gain rather than to a burden. It is arbitrary, of course, to regard the 1939 level of activities as their normal level. Aside from this, it is misleading to disregard the fact that the past defense effort is one of the determinants of future war costs. We should realize that the aggregate burden involved in reaching the objectives of the present war would probably have been diminished by more complete mobilization in the initial stage.

CHAPTER III

The Real Burden of the War

● *The consumption level and the war program.*—The American consumption flow of 1941 was considerably in excess of that of any preceding year and was substantially higher than will be the consumption flow of future war years. The value of ultimate consumption services presumably approximated 75 billions for the calendar year 1941. Economists of the Bureau of Research and Statistics of the O.P.M. have estimated total consumer expenditures for 1941 at 69 billions in 1940 prices.[1] Considering that from 1940 to 1941 the cost of living rose by about 6 per cent, the same flow of commodities and services to ultimate consumers would certainly exceed 70 billions in the actual 1941 prices. Recently the Department of Commerce estimated the 1941 consumption at 73.8 billions in current prices.[2]

It seems that the government plans to allocate to the war during the fiscal year ending with June, 1943, a flow of commodities and services corresponding to about 50 per cent of national income at market prices. "National income at market prices" exceeds "national income at factor costs"[3] by the yield of such federal, state, and local taxes as are paid by or through business firms. These taxes figure as costs in the accounts of firms, and consequently the net output concept corresponding to national income at factor costs implies that a value equal to these tax yields has been used up in the production of other

---
[1] *Estimated Distribution of Civilian Expenditures*, 1940, 1941, 1942 (see fn. 2, p. 25).
[2] Milton Gilbert, "War Expenditures and National Production," *Survey of Current Business*, March, 1942.
[3] National income at factor costs is the sum total of the earnings of the factors of production, including undistributed net corporate earnings. It equals the value of the net output of commodities and services produced, in a sense to be indicated in the text.

items of output. In reality, the commodities and services purchased by the government with these amounts are just like other government services allocated to war or nonwar purposes and not calculated as an accounting cost of enterprise. From our point of view it is necessary, therefore, to add these tax revenues to national income at factor costs in order to arrive at the value of the service flow, part of which the government allocates to the war.[4] According to recent estimates published by Gilbert and Bangs, the appropriate addition amounts to 9.6 billions for 1939, 11.8 billions for 1940, and 17.6 billions for 1941.[5] The magnitude including these tax yields, or rather the magnitude from which these tax yields are not subtracted, is usually referred to as national income at market prices because market values include the taxes under consideration whereas factor earnings do not. National income at current market prices was 80.4 billions in 1939, 89.1 billions in 1940, and 112.3 billions in 1941. These figures measure net output, in the sense of "net of duplications," if government-acquired commodities and services, other than those truly instrumental to some specific process of production, are not conceived as being used up in the production of other items of current output. Net output will be interpreted in this sense throughout the present chapter.

If a flow corresponding to 50 per cent of national income at market prices had been allocated to the war in the calendar year 1941, then the value of consumption would have fallen short of 50 billions. Fifty per cent of the 1941 national income at market prices may be valued at 56 billions. Some fraction of the resources allocated to the war could, however, be supplied by the undermaintenance of the existing stock of real capital,

---

[4] Cf. A. C. Pigou, *Economics of Welfare*, 1924, chap. iii. Professor Pigou's discussion of the national dividend leads one to conclude that the relevant income concept to be considered during a war period is the net national income at market prices plus the amount of capital consumption. Mr. Gilbert gives a very clear discussion of the point in the March, 1942, issue of the *Survey of Current Business*.

[5] *Survey of Current Business*, May, 1942, p. 12.

The Real Burden of the War

that is, by capital consumption. On the other hand, allowance should be made for private investment outlays on plant, equipment, and working capital in war industries. It seems likely that at a mature stage of the war effort capital consumption in the privately financed segment of the economy would outweigh private war investment. If the possible rate of capital consumption is estimated at about 50 per cent of the normal depreciation of the durable stock, and some additional capital consumption is assumed for disinvestment from inventories, a figure of about 8 billions would result. Private war investment would offset some portion of this capital consumption, but it is quite conceivable that the net balance of private disinvestment could be at a rate of about 5 billions for several years.[6] Much the greater part of the war investment is publicly financed and consequently is included in the estimates of war expenditures. Taking account of the possible rate of capital consumption, slightly over 60 billions would, therefore, have remained for human consumption and for nonwar services acquired by the federal government and by state and local governments. Government-acquired nonwar services may be valued at slightly over 12 billions for 1941;[7] consequently, about 48 billions would have remained for human consumption. This is less by one-third than was the actual consumption of 1941 and less by one-fourth than was the 1939 consumption in 1941 prices.

In reality the situation in the fiscal year 1943 ("fiscal '43") will probably be less severe since aggregate real output is still rising. By the time the 50-per cent ratio is reached, more commodities and services will be produced than in 1941. This rise will probably increase the available consumption flow beyond the level just calculated.

It has been pointed out in the preceding chapter that the rise in industrial production has slowed down substantially in the

---

[6] Disinvestment from inventories might be confined to a short period, yet the rate of new war investment might also decline in later stages.

[7] Gilbert, *loc. cit.*

course of 1941. In the second half of the year the percentage rise in industrial production did not amount to more than about 5 per cent, which is less than half the rise of the preceding six-month period.[8] If it were reasonable to assume that this declining trend of the rate of growth would continue unimpeded, then one should expect the future rise in aggregate real output to be negligible. Extrapolating the recent trend might lead to the expectation of a yearly increase in industrial production not exceeding a rate of about 5 per cent. Since industrial production has in the past, proved to be much more flexible than real output as a whole, one might expect on this basis a negligible rise in aggregate real output. The trend, however, will presumably not continue unimpeded.

A rise in average weekly working hours per empoyed person is one of the developments which might lead to higher output levels than those to be derived from extrapolating recent trends. In the two-year period from the summer of 1939 to the summer of 1941, average weekly hours rose by almost 10 per cent in manufacturing industries as a whole and by about 12 per cent in the durable-goods industries. In the second half of 1941 there was practically no change.[9] It could not be held that the weekly labor performance for the war effort has reached an optimum level. Toward the end of 1941 average weekly hours were between 41 and 42 for manufacturing as a whole, and around 43 for durable manufactures. It should be added,

[8] See table 7 in the Appendix.
[9] The *average hours worked per week* were as follows:

		Average hours			Percentage increase, 1939–1941		
		June	July	August	June	July	August
Manufacturing	1939	37.3	36.7	38.0	10.7	9.8	7.9
	1941	41.3	40.3	41.0			
Durable goods	1939	37.4	36.2	38.4	15.2	14.6	10.9
	1941	43.1	41.5	42.6			

Average weekly hours for June, 1941, 41.3; for December, 1941, 41.2.
SOURCE: *Federal Reserve Bulletin.*

The Real Burden of the War   45

however, that in some of the typical war industries the average exceeded 50 hours.[10] For industry as a whole this can hardly be considered an optimum wartime effort. There might as yet be a roughly 15-per cent reserve in working hours. In other words, if appropriate policies are applied, working hours might conceivably rise by about 15 per cent on the average and then be stabilized at that higher level. In addition, employment, that is, the number of employed persons, may in the future increase, especially if employment in the military and naval forces is included. This latter item should be included because all services produced by the government are included in the aggregate output of commodities and services of which 50 per cent is to be allocated to the war. But the appropriate upward correction for output on account of increased employment would not seem to be very significant. So far as persons heretofore unemployed, or heretofore not regarded as part of the "labor force," are put to work, their productivity is likely to be low; and so far as workers are shifted into the armed forces, there is a net decline in the "value of output" because the services rendered in the armed forces are valued at a cost which is less than that in private enterprise. It is true, on the other hand, that the shifting of labor from nondurable- to durable-goods industries is associated with increased "productivity," since value output per man-hour is higher in the durable-goods industries. Yet, on the whole, there seems no good reason to assume that by lengthening hours and increasing employment the total output at constant market prices could be raised by more than about 20 per cent beyond the 1941 level. Moreover, it is likely that complete utilization of this reserve would take much longer than a year, since, in the period in which the economic war machinery is being built up, friction resulting in less than complete utilization is unavoidable.

From the outbreak of the war in Europe to the present time there has been no consistent trend in the manufacturing indus-

---

[10] *Survey of Current Business*, September, 1941, table 4, p. 16.

tries either in the direction of an increase or a decrease in manhour output. In manufacturing as a whole, output rose faster than labor-hour input in the first months after the outbreak of the war in Europe. Then for several months both output and labor-hour input declined slightly. Since the summer months

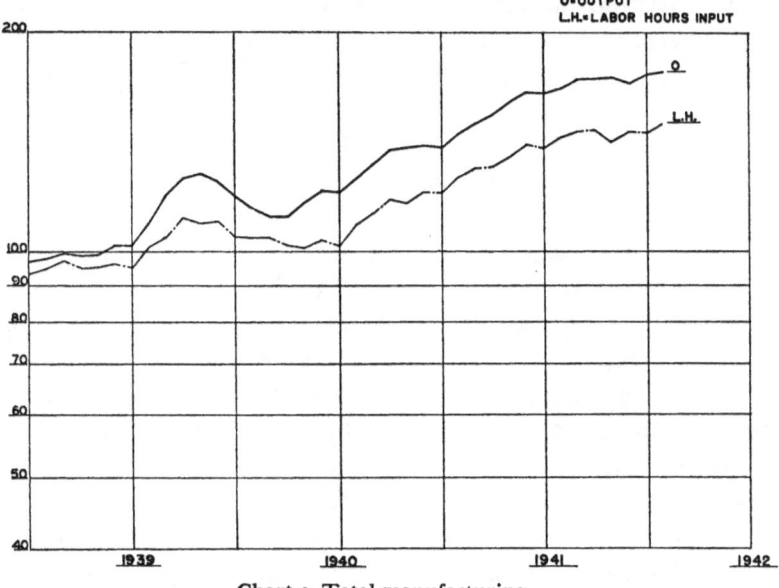

Chart 3. Total manufacturing.

of 1940 there has been no significant difference between the rate of change in output and labor-hour input. In the durable-goods industries viewed separately the situation is similar. These tendencies can be read from charts 3 and 4, where the slope of the O line shows the proportionate increase in output per unit of time and the slope of the LH line shows the proportionate increase in labor hours per unit of time.

Charts relating to several industries are given in the Appendix. In one of the industries examined (Textiles and Products) there has recently been a marked tendency for output to rise in a higher proportion than that in which labor hours have risen; in other industries this tendency seems to have been

The Real Burden of the War

absent or weak, although lessening of the quantity of work because of long hours and low-quality workers had not been typical of those industries in the past. It is hard to draw conclusions regarding the future from trends like these, but it does not seem likely that, if the available reserve in labor hours

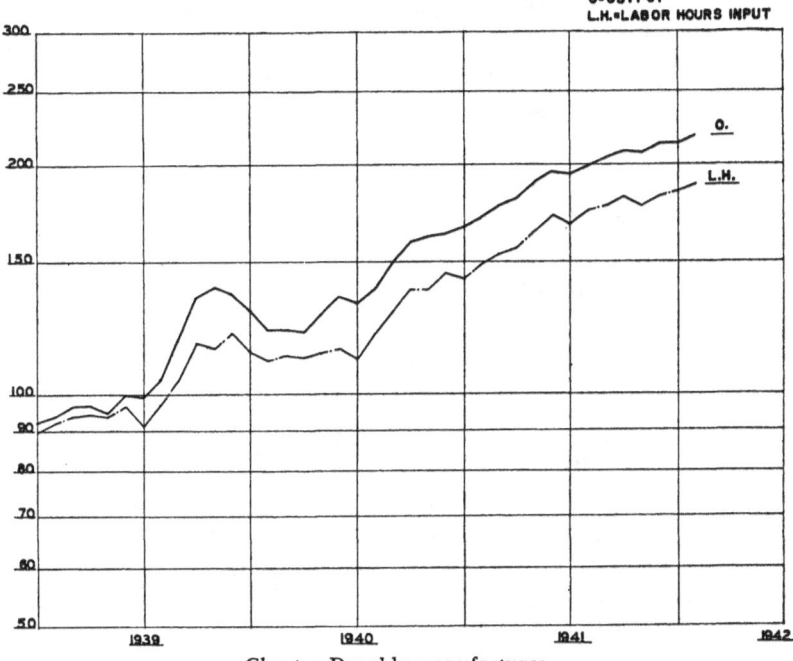

Chart 4. Durable manufactures.

were to be fully exhausted (which undoubtedly means long hours and low-quality workers), output could increase at a rate equal to the rate of increase in labor-hours.

Previously, we concluded that if all reserves were to be exhausted, the aggregate output of the economy might conceivably rise by a further margin of about 20 per cent. Should average weekly hours actually be increased by 15 per cent, as was considered above, and should the available labor force be expanded to include women now unoccupied, total labor-hour input could be increased by considerably more than 20 per cent. Yet, should labor hours be increased in the highest possible proportion, then output would very likely increase in a smaller proportion than labor hours. The slope of the O lines on our charts would then have to become smaller in relation to the slope of he LH lines. As to the shifting of resources from one industry to the other, shifting from nondurable- to durable-goods industries tends to increase value output per man-hour, but shifting from private industries to the armed forces tends to offset this increase.

We have seen that if aggregate real output were stabilized at its 1941 level, the annual rate of consumption would, at the peak of the war effort, fall short of 50 billions in 1941 prices. If within a period of two years net output at constant market prices could be increased by 20 per cent beyond the 1941 level of 112 billions, and if 50 per cent of the increase should become available for consumption, then the consumption flow compatible with the war program would rise to almost 60 billions at 1941 prices. This is in excess of the previously calculated level of 48 billions by about 11 to 12 billions. The addition which could be achieved during the fiscal year 1943 would, however, presumably be smaller because in a period of rapid change requiring complex adjustments, it is impossible to utilize all the potential reserves fully; and it is very likely that in the event of a long war the further increase in output, after 1943, would be wholly allocated to war purposes. Therefore, 55 billions at 1941 prices seems to be a reasonable estimate for the consumption flow at the peak of the war program contemplated now. The necessary curtailment from the 1941 level would then be about 25 per cent and the margin by which wartime consumption would fall short of the 1939 consumption level would be around 15 per cent at constant prices.

Professor Pigou's four categories.—It may be useful to fit this conclusion into the framework presented by Professor Pigou in his *Political Economy of War.* Pigou suggests that the resources used for war may be grouped into four categories cor-

The Real Burden of the War

responding to their uses, if they were used at all, prior to the war. Ordinarily, some part of the war resources was not previously utilized (or, it may be added, was nonexistent[11]); another part is diverted from new capital formation; still another part is diverted from the maintenance of the real capital stock; and finally, some part is set free for the war sector of the economy through the reduction of ultimate human consumption. These categories are defined in such a way that all resources can be grouped in one of the four classes. Not all wars, of course, need draw on each of the four classes of resources. In fact, we have seen that in the period of American nonbelligerency all war resources of this country were derived from the first of the four categories. Yet experience shows that the major wars of modern times ultimately do draw on all four of these sources.

Our previous conclusions can be fitted into this framework. If the real output flow of the base year 1939, as measured in market prices, is arbitrarily called "100 units," then the current output flow may be said to have risen by 1941 to about 130 units at constant prices.[12] It seems reasonable to expect that at the peak of the war effort now contemplated the annual real output flow will at least approximate 145 units; and full utilization of the reserves previously considered might even lift the output flow of the later stages of the war period to 155 units. We assume that in the fiscal year 1943 a flow corresponding to about 50 per cent of output will be allocated to the war. By this time net output in constant market prices may be about 145 units. Later it may conceivably rise even higher; but it seems reasonable to assume that if by that time the Axis is not yet defeated the further increase would be wholly diverted to war

---

[11] Resources acquired through capital formation out of current output during the war were previously "nonexistent." Resources acquired by conquest also constitute a net addition to the resources of the country under consideration. Pigou's classification relates to a given aggregate stock of resources.

[12] Net national income at market prices was about 80 billions in 1939 and 112 billions in 1941. If the latter figure is deflated by the rise in prices from 1939 to 1941, net national income becomes about 105 billions, which is 30 per cent above the 1939 level.

production, so that consumption would not increase in the further course of the war. One-half of 145 units amounts to 73 units, which would be used for war purposes in the fiscal year 1943. Possibly about 7 units of the 72–73 could be taken out of the excess of capital consumption over private war investment—these 7 units corresponding to the 5 billions previously estimated; hence about 78–79 units would remain for consumption and for nonwar services acquired by the federal, state, and municipal divisions of government. The government-acquired nonwar services, the value of which is likely to decline somewhat, may account for about 14 units, leaving for consumption 65 units. As against the 65 units here derived, the consumption of 1939 amounted to about 76 units and that of 1941 to about 86 units. The consumption flow of the lowest depression level (1933) was 56 units.

On the 145 level of output this would mean that about 60 per cent of the war resources would be supplied by increased output, the remainder by the curtailment of consumption and, in a somewhat higher measure, by the substitution of capital consumption for the prewar net capital formation.[13] It should be emphasized, however, that if 1941 rather than 1939 were chosen as a "base year," a different relation would result. The obvious reason is that a significant part of the increase in output had already occurred by 1941, while consumption had risen, rather than declined, in the two years between the outbreak of the war in Europe and the attack on Pearl Harbor. If 1941 is chosen as a starting point, then more than half the *additional* resources to be allocated to the war will have to be supplied by the diminution of consumption.

---

[13] *The Economist* has estimated that in Great Britain the resources now used for war production come from the following sources in the following proportions:

> Increased production .... 23 per cent
> Drafts on capital .... 52 per cent
> Reduced consumption .... 25 per cent

Drafts on capital include capital consumption plus the cessation of prewar capital formation. See "The Shadow of the Budget," *The Economist*, January 3, 1942.

Numerical comparisons: changes in distribution.—A quantitative comparison of the consumption flows of different periods may become misleading if no account is taken of changes which occur in the composition of consumption and in the distribution of income. This qualification to numerical comparisons of real flows is of general validity, but it acquires special significance in the comparison here under consideration. It follows from the preceding analysis that the per-capita consumption compatible with the present war program may be somewhat in excess of the deepest consumption level of the great depression, but that the margin of excess falls short of 10 per cent. This does not, however, imply that the consumption standards of the war period will be similar to those of the great depression. Even if we were comparing two normal years, we would have to remember the limitations of the method of comparing real magnitudes by correcting changes in money flows for price changes. Such limitations become exceedingly narrow when a peacetime year is compared with a war year. There are two reasons for this, and they are not entirely unrelated to one another. First, the distribution of wartime consumption among various groups of the population may become very different from what it was either in 1932–33 or in the late 1930's. Second, the difference in the physical composition of the consumption flow will also be much more significant than are typical changes within the same historical period of economic development. These two phenomena are associated with each other since different groups of the population consume different things. However, in times of war the changed composition of consumer demand is not the main determinant of the physical composition of the reduced consumption flow.

Unless the monetary situation gets out of control, it is reasonable to expect that the distribution of the consumption flow between the different income and wealth brackets of the population will be less unequal than is usually true in periods of low consumption. Low levels of consumption normally coincide with substantial unemployment. The employed part of the population taken as a whole is also typically worse off in a major depression than during the prosperity phase of the cycle, but its standard of living declines by a much smaller margin than that of the unemployed. This circumstance gives rise to a type of inequality characteristic of depressions. There does not exist any single meaningful measure for the degree of equality—or the degree of inequality—of income distribution. Nor does there exist any measure for the equality or inequality of the distribution of consumption—which is a somewhat different matter since the income recipients of the various income brackets consume different fractions of their incomes. A given distribution of income or of consumption may be "more nearly equal" than another distribution in one sense and "more unequal" in another sense. The typical income distribution of depressions is highly "unequal" in the sense that the number of persons earning small fractions of the average income is substantially increased. This is mainly a consequence of large-scale unemployment, and hence war periods of low consumption should not be characterized by this type of inequality. Normal periods of high employment, on the other hand, are characterized by another type of inequality. In phases of prosperity the share of income flowing to those who earn high multiples of the average is typically increased. The question arises whether in a war economy this other type of inequality is likely to reach the extent which characterizes normal prosperity phases.

To what extent these inequalities of income arise in a war period depends largely on government policies. One might say, of course, that the appropriate fiscal policies could cut down these inequalities in a peacetime expansion as well as in a war boom. There is an important difference, however. A normal expansion is typically much more sensitive than is the upward trend of a war period. High profits in a normal expansion could probably not be eliminated without suppressing the expansion itself in an early stage. Wartime production, however, will be continued even if profits after taxes are not allowed to rise to boom levels. The stimulus provided by the profit motive should not be entirely eliminated from a war economy. But, while highly progressive taxation might prevent business recovery and prosperity in normal times, a policy of keeping profits from rising to boom levels does not necessarily undermine economic efficiency in times of war. Consequently, in times of war the appropriate fiscal policies might produce an income distribution characterized by absence of the typical inequalities of depression, and yet not show typical inequalities of booms to the same degree as is usual in peacetime prosperity. Moreover, even if some of the inequalities of boom periods prove inevitable, the distribution of consumption need not display these inequalities to the same degree. Rationing of consumers' goods is a means by which the relationship between income distribution and the distribution of consumption is weakened. To the extent to which rationing is effective, inequalities of income are incompletely translated into inequalities of consumption.

Hence, if the monetary situation remains under reasonably effective control and certain equalitarian measures such as progressive taxation and rationing are applied successfully, it should be possible to reduce inequalities not merely as compared with peacetime periods of depression but also as compared with normal years of high business activity. The distribution pattern of the reduced consumption flow may be expected to be different from the usual peacetime patterns. We have here one set of factors seriously limiting the meaning of numerical comparisons, so far as they relate to peacetime and to war aggregates.

Numerical comparisons: changes in physical composition.— Changes in the physical composition of the consumption flow constitute another set of factors to be considered in the same context. These changes must be expected to become significant. It is obvious that comparisons of real flows lose much of their meaning if they relate to aggregates of markedly different composition.

Normally, in times of low consumption, the degree of curtailment of the different specific items within the consumption flow depends mainly upon how the demand functions for the various products shift downward. In depressions it is the shrinkage of incomes which leads to the reduction of consumption. The distribution of the reduced income flow between various groups of the population and the income elasticity of individual demands for different products may be considered the main determinants of the degree of curtailment to which the various items within aggregate consumption are subject. This, generally speaking, is not true of wartime consumption. Whether money incomes disposable for consumption rise, remain unchanged, or decline depends on how the war is financed. But regardless of what happens to disposable money incomes, the specific character of the real shortages occasioned by the war demand of the government becomes a highly significant determinant of the relative curtailment of the different consumption items. These real shortages are produced by the commandeering of resources for war production through priority regulations or, even more effectively, through direct allocation. The specific shortages may reflect themselves in the relative rise of the prices of those consumers' goods the supply of which is curtailed by the diversion of specific resources to war; or, alternatively, the government may ration the consumers' goods the output of which must be curtailed. But in either event the relative changes in the conditions of supply become the main determinants of what may be called the breakdown of the curtailment into specific commodities and services. Only to the extent to which the hostilities themselves and the requirements of war production do not effect the supplies of different commodities can the breakdown of aggregate demand be allowed to determine the composition of the reduced consumption flow. This is a significant difference between wartime and peacetime periods of low consumption.

The hope seems justified that the specific character of the shortages will be much less onerous here than in most of the warring countries. In fact, it may not be an overstatement to say that the relatively favorable character of the "breakdown" of wartime consumption promises to be one of the most conspicuous advantages of this country over the enemy nations. The commodities "directly competing with war production" are largely in the nature of "conveniences" rather than of "necessities." The same is true of the items normally imported from what now are war zones. A substantial share of the curtailment will fall in the category of durable consumers' goods. A marked reduction will have to take place in other fields as well, but it seems likely that the shortages will not reach down into the field of necessities in the narrower sense. There seems to be no reason to assume that the population will be ill-fed or ill-clothed, although internal migration may continue to cause acute local housing shortages for some time to come.

That durable consumers' goods are not necessities in any immediately pressing way is obvious. It should be added, however, that curtailment of the consumption of these commodities is an ambiguous notion. Two phenomena falling under this heading must be distinguished from each other. To cut off the supply of new durable consumers' goods is one thing; to prevent the public from using its existing stock of these commodities is another. The burden of not being able to buy new durable goods is much smaller than that of being unable to use one's given stock. Both the replacement and the current use of durable consumers' goods may, in a reasonable sense, be classified as mere "conveniences," but postponing replacement is a much smaller inconvenience than is refraining from use.

It should be emphasized that the substantial rise in the purchase of new durable consumers' goods after 1939—and especially in 1941[14]— definitely reduces the burden entailed in the mere postponement of replacements. In fact, part of this burden will be only apparent, since part of the replacements which ordinarily would have been undertaken in years to come were actually made at an earlier date in the anticipation of later shortages. Yet the lack of availability of new durable consumers' goods will force some of the population to refrain from using new goods rather than merely defer their replacement. Individuals and families not possessing any stock of a certain type of durable consumers' goods are more adversely affected if they normally would have become purchasers of that specific commodity in the course of the next few years; newly established households are an example of this. Moreover, the line between deferring replacements and refraining from use tends to be gradually wiped out as time passes. A given stock of durable consumers' goods cannot be used indefinitely. Yet, on any reasonable assumption of the duration of the war, there should be a substantial difference for the majority of the population between lack of availability of new durable goods and the necessity of giving up using these goods.

The shortages which may lead to limiting the use of durable consumers' goods are partly of the same kind as those necessitating the postponement of replacements. Partly, however, the character of the shortages leading to these two consequences are different. A shortage of raw materials used in the production of automobiles, refrigerators, or washing machines will lead to curtailment or cessation of the production of these articles. A severer shortage of the same materials may make it necessary to requisition existing stocks. The stocks may then be used as "producers' goods" in the war industries, including the armed forces; or, in especially severe circumstances, they may be scrapped and used as raw materials. Often, however, limitations of use are consequences of a different set of factors. There may occur a shortage in commodities needed for the

---

[14] See table 2, chap. ii.

operating of certain durable goods, such as the present shortage in rubber tires or the gasoline shortage in certain areas of the country.

On the basis of O.P.M. estimates, it seems likely that the complete elimination of the new output flow of durable consumers' goods plus a rather far-reaching reduction of the current use of automobiles would correspond roughly to a 10–12-per cent curtailment of consumption from its 1941 level. The expenditures on items usually included in the category of durable consumers' goods are estimated for 1941 at almost 12 per cent of aggregate consumers' expenditures. This includes the running cost of automobiles. If one-half of these running costs is subtracted, a ratio of roughly 10 per cent results.[15] This ratio should, however, probably be corrected slightly upward. The O.P.M. estimate, derived from the estimates of the National Resources Committee for an earlier year, includes the amounts spent on used as well as on new cars but values the new cars at a price from which trade-in allowances are deducted. For the twelve-month period July, 1935–July, 1936, to which the estimate of the National Resources Committee applies, the aggregate value of new car purchases by consumers, calculated without deduction of trade-in allowances, seems to have been somewhat in excess of the value of the new plus used car purchases as calculated by the National Resources Committee. For our purposes the total value of the flow of new durable consumers' goods to ultimate consumers is the relevant figure. One-half of the running costs of automobiles added to this sum probably has exceeded 10 per cent of consumers' expenditures for 1941.

---

[15] In 1941 8.2 per cent of total expenditures was estimated as spent on automobiles and 3.0 per cent on household furnishings. To the sum of these two figures must be added a small fraction of the 3.6 per cent spent on recreation to include such items as radios. This would give a total of roughly 12 per cent. The National Resources Committee, in *Consumer Expenditures in the United States*, has estimated running costs of automobiles at about one-half of total expenditures on automobiles. This would amount to about 4 per cent, and one-half of running costs at about 2 per cent. Thus the total of 12 per cent is reduced to about 10 per cent.

It follows from our previous considerations that even the complete elimination of the output of new durable consumers' goods and a substantial curtailment of the use of existing automobiles would fall distinctly short of the necessary measure of consumption curtailment. Roughly, 12 per cent of the 1941 consumption corresponds to less than 10 billion dollars. We have seen previously that the value, in 1941 prices, of the consumption flow compatible with the peak level of the war effort now contemplated will hardly exceed 55 billions. The actual value of consumer expenditures in 1941 was close to 74 billions. The necessary curtailment would therefore correspond to about 20 billions in 1941 prices, and the contribution of durable consumers' goods (including their "running costs") to this reduction could not exceed 50 per cent. About 10 billions would have to be taken from the fields of semidurable and perishable consumers' goods and the degree of curtailment would be on the order of 15 per cent for consumers' goods other than "durable." The burden will be somewhat reduced by the fact that several million consumers will be shifted over to the armed forces. To this extent civilian consumption tends to decline automatically.

Recently, various authors have forecast that the consumption of the fiscal year 1943 would be higher than the level resulting from the foregoing calculations. It was estimated that the consumption of nondurable commodities would be reduced but slightly below the 1941 level. These estimates imply, however, that the economic war effort will lag behind the plans relating to war expenditures and to the share of output to be allocated to the war. In the foregoing pages I was concerned with the consumption flow compatible with the plans outlined in official announcements, such as that of the Budget Director on April 24 and that of the Secretary of the Treasury on July 2, 1942. It may be that these plans will not be fully accomplished until a somewhat later date; but it is to be hoped that they will. The lagging of war production behind the program would suggest the necessity of reducing the standards of convertability of "civilian" equipment into equipment producing for the war: convertability is frequently a matter of degree, that is, a matter of the amount of civilian output to be sacrificed per unit of additional war output. It would also suggest the necessity of allocating labor to the war industries.

Other factors affecting appraisal of future burden.—However rough these calculations may be, they show clearly that the consumption burden must become substantial in magnitude. In the preceding chapter we have noted some of the circumstances which render all quantitative measures of the economic war burden more or less misleading. There I have stressed those complicating circumstances which have to be taken into account in connection with the period between the outbreak of the war in Europe and the attack on Pearl Harbor. If the future burden is to be appraised, further circumstances must also be emphasized. The consumption burden is not the entire burden, because resources which otherwise would have been used for new capital formation, and some resources which otherwise would have served the purpose of capital maintenance, will also be diverted to wartime use. These are significant items and they have a characteristic which the consumption burden does not possess unless it affects the state of health of the population. The discontinuation of the normal growth of real capital (in peacetime industries) and the undermaintenance of the capital stock have a future aspect as well as a present one. Capital can always be conceived as "present value" or alternatively as a "stream of future yields." Capital inherently possesses both these aspects. To the extent to which war consumes capital it reduces a future income stream of indefinite length.

It is impossible to estimate the amount of capital formation which will be suppressed by the war. This depends on what capital formation would have amounted to had the war not broken out. If we assume arbitrarily that capital formation would have continued approximately at its 1939 rate and that the capital consumption (undermaintenance) imposed upon the civilian sector will amount to roughly one-half of the normal depreciation, then the loss in capital stock caused by the war would be at a yearly rate of about 12 to 15 billions at 1941 prices. It is true, however, that the capital invested in war industries need not be entirely lost for peacetime purposes. A substantial part of this capital may conceivably be changed into "civilian" equipment at some cost.

Even more intangible are the effects of the war on the economic conditions of the ensuing decades. The social costs involved in postwar adjustments are, of course, also a war burden. Yet, if it will be possible to establish conditions in which economic activities can be carried on without substantial disturbances over a wide area, the war may turn out not merely to have averted an attempt at world conquest but also to have given rise to a net economic gain as compared with prewar conditions.

The loss in "human capital" should also not be left out of account. We do not primarily regard human beings as means of production, and consequently the economic aspect of the wartime casualties is their least significant aspect; nevertheless, human beings are productive agencies as well as consumers, and wars do impose a burden on communities by diminishing and deteriorating their stock of "human capital" as well as by consuming capital in the ordinary sense.

CHAPTER IV

The Financing of Defense Prior to Pearl Harbor

● *Expansionary financing vs. induced consumption and induced investment.*—The rise in the real output flow of the American economy after the outbreak of the war in Europe was accompanied by a substantial increase in the flow of money spending. In fact, it is unlikely that the aggregate real output flow would have risen at a rate approximating its actual rate of increase had the flow of money spending been kept constant.

A rise in real output implies a declining price level if the money flow remains unchanged. In principle, a process characterized by expanding real output and a declining price level is quite conceivable. In reality, we have to a limited extent experienced such a process. In the late 1920's, for example, prices exhibited a slight downward tendency while output was rising rapidly. Yet a substantial decline of the general price level gives rise to frictions which are not easily overcome. A rise in the output flow by about 30 per cent in the course of two years would have created a substantial pressure on the price level, had the money flow remained unchanged. Flexible monetary policies were, in all probability, a necessary condition of this rise in physical production.

A reasonable monetary policy would have increased the supply of money even if from the outset it had been the objective of the authorities to prevent a rise in consumption. Such a policy would conceivably have aimed at stabilizing incomes net of taxes in the attempt to prevent an increase in consumption spending. Moreover, it would have prevented an increase in bank loans for nondefense purposes. But a policy aiming at maximum physical output would have brought about a rise in aggregate money spending, including public and private expenditures on defense commodities, even if it had attempted to stabilize or curtail the flow of human consumption and of nondefense investment.

In the general discussion of this topic there frequently arises a confusion between the probable effects of alternative monetary and fiscal policies on aggregate output, on the one hand, and the probable effects of alternative policies on consumption, on the other. Methods of financing a defense program in which the creation of new money is involved are likely to stimulate a rise in aggregate output so long as the economy has a substantial stock of unutilized resources at its disposal, whereas the continuation of expansionary financing is likely to exhaust itself more and more in raising prices as the aggregate supply of commodities and services loses its elasticity. But an increase in the supply of money does not necessarily stimulate the production of consumers' goods. A government, for example, might borrow from banks part of the funds to be expended on defense and might raise tax revenues with a lag, so as to force the consumer to spend his additional money income on taxes rather than on consumption goods.[1] Such a policy would balance the budget with a lag,[2] although it would create no balance between simultaneous revenues and expenditures. The revenue of a period would balance with the expenditures of the previous period, but would fall short of the expenditures of the "present" period. The appropriate way to reach this objective presumably would be that of raising the tax liabilities of the public simultaneously by the full amount of the rise in aggregate money income. The lag in balancing revenues with expenditures would reflect (a) the possible lag between Treasury spending and the formation of net incomes (via intermedi-

---

[1] In principle we should add: "except for that part of the additional money income which goes into additional savings." In the event of noninflationary war finance this qualification would presumably be unimportant.

[2] With the same qualification as is contained in footnote [1] above.

The Financing of Defense

ate stages), and (b) the necessarily existing lag between the accrual and the collection of taxes. In order to prevent the formation of a revolving consumption fund during the second of these two lags, income taxes would probably have to be deducted at the source. If in times of rising real output and of expanding money flows nondefense expenditures are to be curtailed (not merely stabilized), the budget should even be overbalanced with a lag although underbalanced in simultaneous terms. In these circumstances the tax liabilities of the public should increase by more than the rise in money incomes. It is important to realize that no contradiction is involved in this proposition, because, as was pointed out in the introductory chapter, there is a difference between (a) letting money income rise but conducting the increase (or more) back to the Treasury before it is spent on consumption, and (b) not letting money income rise.

To say that the methods of financing the defense program were expansionary from the outset is not the same thing as to say that defense outlays gave rise to an increased consumption and to induced nondefense investment. Expansionary financing—that is, financing involving monetary expansion—was presumably necessary to obtaining a substantial rise in aggregate real output. The increase in consumption spending, on the other hand, as well as the increase in nondefense investment, reflects the circumstance that an appreciable part of the previously unutilized resources was taken up by the civilian sector rather than by the defense industries.

Some of the data referred to in the preceding chapters lend plausibility to the assumption that the endeavor to maximize real output was not the sole reason for expansionary financing. It was pointed out that since early 1941 both the wholesale price level and the cost of living have shown a marked upward trend. Moreover, since the summer of 1941 the rise in industrial production has been slow while prices have continued to rise. There would be no plausibility in the assumption that this was necessary, or that it was deemed to be necessary, in order to prevent a less favorable trend in the development of real output. A downward pressure on the price level might create an unfavorable trend for the real output flow, and a slightly rising price level may conceivably stimulate the expansion of

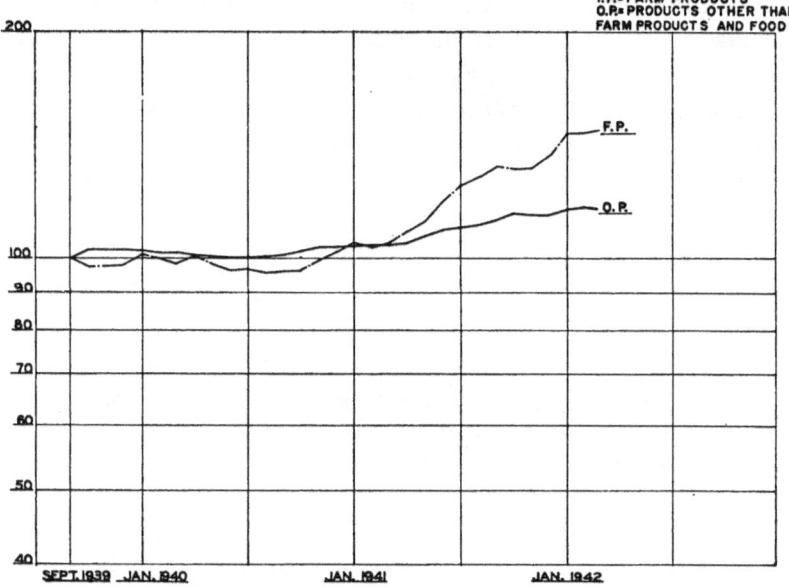

Chart 5. Prices of farm and nonfarm products. Converted to September, 1939 = 100.

production. Even in an economy in which priorities, allocations, and public investment direct resources into the required channels, and in which the government has means to enforce the utilization of idle stocks, it is inopportune to create a downward pressure on the price level and thereby to increase the difficulties involved in the task of allocating resources. But a sharp rise in the general price level is neither a necessary nor a welcome stimulus. Furthermore, it is clear that the shifts *within* the general price level were not, for the most part, of a kind to promote expediency in the defense program. Farm prices were and are the conspicuous leaders in the race. The ratio of farm prices to other prices has shifted substantially in favor of the former. It is clearly not, however, the aim of the government to shift resources from other industries to farming.

Expansionary financing, as opposed to induced consumption and to induced nondefense investment, did serve the purposes of the defense program since it promoted a considerable rise in real output. Furthermore, some degree of expansionary financing is still appropriate since real output has not as yet entirely ceased to rise. But the degree of expansionary financing was and is greater than that which would be determined by these considerations. The amount of expansionary financing was and is greatly influenced by the limitations to which other methods of financing are subject. In principle, expansionary financing comprises borrowing from banks, borrowing from previously accumulated idle balances, and such taxation as results in the depletion of idle balances. There are strong indications that idle balances were increased rather than depleted up to the time of the Pearl Harbor attack,[3] with the result that expansionary financing was, in practice, confined to borrowing from banks. The amount borrowed from banks was greatly influenced by the fact that the Administration did not want to—or conceivably could not—press taxation beyond certain limits which changed with changing conditions, and by the fact that borrowing from the public (i.e., from lenders other than banks) was limited by the voluntary demand of the public for government securities. These considerations do not determine the amount of expansionary borrowing in any rigid manner. To say that because of these circumstances the amount borrowed from banks is merely residual would be an overstatement. The effort to press taxation may, for example, have increased in the course of the last two years. It may be true—although it is by no means obviously true—that, as time has passed, the degree of taxation has not merely increased, but has also more and more closely approximated the politically

---
[3] See below, p. 77.

feasible degree in each subsequent stage. It is impossible, however, to verify this. The effort to borrow from the public rather than from banks has obviously increased, and the absolute amount of borrowing from the public has risen substantially; but the increase has not been sufficient to prevent a considerable upward pressure in the price level since the early months of 1941.

In spite of increased taxation and increased borrowing from the public, the rate of new money creation has risen appreciably since the outbreak of the war in Europe. In the fiscal year ending with June, 1940 ("fiscal 1940"), about 5 billions of new money came into existence. In the next fiscal year ("fiscal 1941") the supply of money rose by about 7.5 billions to slightly more than 48 billions. "Money" is here defined as including (1) demand deposits other than domestic interbank deposits and (2) hand-to-hand currency other than that held by the Treasury and by banks. The inclusion of time deposits and of savings accounts would not change our figures substantially, as far as the increase in the stock of money is concerned. These balances did not rise much.[4]

The first fiscal year.—Up to the start of the American defense program, in June, 1940, monetary expansion was but indirectly related to the war. As can be seen from table 1 in the Appendix, American industrial production rose appreciably in the first year of the war in Europe, although the rise became much more substantial in the second year, which roughly coincides with the first year of the American defense program. It can be seen from the same table that, already in the first year of the war, the largest rise occurred in the typical defense industries. The expansion of the period between the outbreak of war and the start of the American defense program should be viewed as the first stage of the American war expansion. But at that time the expansion could not be regarded as a consequent of American government activities.

---
[4] See table 9 in the Appendix.

The Financing of Defense

The increased demand of warring nations for American commodities was the medium through which the "stimulating" impact of the war was mainly transmitted. Table 8 in the Appendix shows the large increase in exports to which the war gave rise in the first year. This stimulus was much greater than could conceivably have arisen from the very slight increase in American defense spending. Subsequently, a high foreign (mainly British) demand for American commodities continued, and so did the rise in exports; but after the summer of 1940 the American defense program became more and more the prime mover. Furthermore, since the spring of 1941, when the Lend-Lease Act was passed, the line between American defense spending and exports has ceased to be distinct. Fiscal expenditures on goods to be "lent and leased" to the United Nations are included in American defense spending.

Between the outbreak of the war in Europe and the summer of 1940, the expenditures of the federal government must be assumed to have had an even smaller part in bringing about the rise in output than would appear from figures relating to defense outlays. The national defense expenditures of the federal government did rise slightly; these outlays amounted to 1.7 billions in the fiscal year 1940 as against 1.2 billions in the previous fiscal year. Yet fiscal revenue also rose slightly and there was some decline in unemployment relief outlays. Hence the excess of expenditures over receipts was about the same in both fiscal years (3.6 billions). This alone does not prove that "deficit financing" failed to rise after the outbreak of the war in Europe. The excess of expenditures over receipts of the federal government does not reflect the amount of the deficit in any meaningful sense. Numerous government agencies are technically excluded from the concept of the "federal government," but from our point of view they should be included. It would obviously be misleading to say that "the deficit" remained unchanged from one year to the other, in case the statement were true only of the federal government in the narrower sense without its being true of the aggregate consisting of the federal government and of its agencies. Some of these agencies, mainly the Reconstruction Finance Corporation and its subsidiaries, now play a very significant part in financing the war program.[5] It is shown in table 10 of the Appendix that the deficit of the aggregate consisting of the federal government and its agencies was 2.1 billions in the last prewar fiscal year, and amounted to about 2.4 billions for the fiscal year 1940. This rise of roughly 300 millions is even slighter than the increase in the "national defense expenditures" of the federal government.

The monetary and real expansion, which occurred up to the fall of France, was a consequence of an increased foreign demand for American commodities, of improved expectations respecting the future demand for armament products, and of a Multiplier Effect. It cannot, however, be viewed as substantially a consequence of American government activities.

The second fiscal year.—In the next fiscal year, that is, in the

---

[5] Financing of industrial facilities for defense is as follows: A large part of the plant expansion occurring in defense industries is government-financed. The government provides funds not merely for those industrial facilities which will be government-owned and government-operated; it also provides funds for facilities to be government-owned and privately operated, and to some extent also for facilities to be privately owned and privately operated. The funds invested in government-owned and government-operated facilities, so-called *plan G.O.* investments, figure among the budget expenditures of the federal government. Under *plan D.P.C.*, government-owned and privately operated facilities are originally financed by the Reconstruction Finance Corporation through its subsidiary the Defense Plant Corporation; but the government in the narrower sense, specifically the Army or the Navy, gradually reimburses these agencies for a substantial share of the funds invested and these reimbursements take place out of budget funds. Under *plan E.P.F.* (Emergency Plant Facilities), some of the privately owned and privately operated facilities also involve public financing, since the Army or the Navy reimburses some of the private producers or their creditors in the course of a five-year period for the amounts invested in defense facilities. Under this last plan the original financing may be undertaken by the Reconstruction Finance Corporation, by a bank, or by the producer himself; the reimbursement, however, takes place out of budget funds. Under plan E.P.F. and plan D.P.C., the private entrepreneur is granted an option which he may exercise at the end of five years either to buy the plant from the government or leave it in government hands. The fourth plan, so-called *plan P.O.*, does not involve government financing of industrial

The Financing of Defense

first year of the American defense program, the deficit of the federal government in the broader sense rose appreciably.[6] Although the deficit did not rise as sharply as did defense outlays, it nevertheless doubled. In the fiscal year 1941 national defense expenditures amounted to 6.1 billions, as against the 1.7 billions of the previous fiscal year. The deficit did not, however, rise by the full amount of this increase, since revenues rose and nondefense expenditures declined. The rise in the deficit of the federal government in the narrower sense amounted to 1.5 billions. If this figure is corrected for the expenditures of the federal agencies, the deficit of the aggregate consisting of the federal government and of its agencies rose by 2.3 billions. This corrected deficit figure rose from 2.4 billions for the fiscal year 1940 to 4.7 billions for fiscal 1941.

It is this increased corrected deficit of 4.7 billions which gave rise to the largest single constituent of the "new money" created during the fiscal year 1941. Almost two-thirds of the borrowing was from banks, which directly caused the investments of banks and the supply of money to increase.[7] The banking

---

facilities. The P.O. facilities are privately owned, privately operated, and privately financed.

It may be concluded from figures published in *Victory* (March 17, 1942) that through December, 1941, slightly more than 80 per cent of all approved defense industrial plant expansion involved the commitment of public funds. It may also be concluded from earlier announcements that most of this 80 per cent is government-owned and government-operated (G.O.), or government-owned and privately operated (D.P.C.), with but a relatively small share falling in the category of privately financed, privately operated, yet government-reimbursed projects (E.P.F.).

In addition to financing industrial facilities, the government agencies under consideration supply credits for working capital on a large scale.

[6] See table 10 in the Appendix.

[7] For the period June, 1940–June, 1941 the percentage of new issues going to banks was 52.1 per cent; to insurance companies, 5.8 per cent; to "other investors," 21.8 per cent; to federal agencies and trust funds, 20.6 per cent. For the period June, 1939–June, 1941 the percentage of new issues going to banks was 47.0 per cent; to insurance companies, 10.6 per cent; to "other investors," 15.9 per cent; and to federal agencies and trust funds, 27.3 per cent. Banks include Federal Reserve banks, member banks, other commercial banks, and mutual savings banks. The holdings of the Federal Reserve banks changed but slightly. The foregoing figures are from *Federal Reserve Bulletins*.

system, including the Federal Reserve banks, increased its holdings of government securities—direct and fully guaranteed[8]—by about 3.5 billions.[9]

At the same time, bank loans also rose at an increased rate. From June, 1940, to June, 1941, the rise in loans outstanding amounted to 3 billions, whereas the rise of the preceding fiscal year did not exceed 1 billion. This rise was to an appreciable degree, although by no means entirely, the consequence of defense investments. A survey conducted by the Board of Governors of the Federal Reserve System indicated that for the period August 21, 1940–April 30, 1941 defense loans accounted for somewhat less than one-half the rise in outstanding commercial loans, so far as member banks of the 101 leading cities were concerned. In loans as well as investments almost the entire increase was due to activities of the member banks. For nonmember banks the rise is exceedingly small.

[8] The fully guaranteed securities are those issued by the government agencies.

[9] This figure corresponds to almost 75 per cent of the previously derived deficit figure. Yet the borrowing was in excess of the deficit since the general fund balance of the government and of the agencies was increased by about 700 million during the fiscal year under consideration. Hence the total borrowing of the government in the broader sense (including agencies) amounted to 5.4 billions and the 3.5 billions, representing the amount borrowed from banks, corresponds to about two-thirds of this aggregate.

The member banks alone purchased 3.4 billions in government securities—direct and fully guaranteed—during the fiscal year 1941. The nonmember commercial banks have increased their holdings of government securities by about 200 millions, and the mutual savings banks by 300 millions. The sum of these purchases amounts, roughly, to 3.9 billions, but the Federal Reserve banks have sold close to 300 millions of direct and fully guaranteed government securities during the same period.

It should be added that the other "investments" of the banks did not change significantly in the course of the fiscal year. There was a slight decline in other investments as a consequence of the fact that nonmember banks decreased their holdings of other securities by more than the equivalent of the small increase which occurred in the holdings of the member banks. All investments of the banking system, excluding the Federal Reserve banks, rose by 3.6 billions, which is less by 300 millions than the rise in their holdings of government securities. In the preceding fiscal year, that is, in fiscal 1940, the investments of all banks other than the Federal Reserve banks rose by no more than 700 millions. This conspicuous rise in the new "investments" of the banks from fiscal 1940 to fiscal 1941 was the main additional expansionary factor in the first year of the defense program.

The Financing of Defense 71

The total rise in the supply of money during the fiscal year under consideration was in excess of the increase in bank loans and investments by 1 to 1½ billions, since the gold inflow was a further source of money creation. The amount of gold certificates held by member banks rose by about 2.6 billions during fiscal 1941. On the other hand, a relatively small fraction of the total increase in bank assets was not associated with an increase in the stock of "money" since it had an increase in time and saving accounts for its counterpart.

It appears from these data that the substantial increase in the supply of money during the fiscal year 1941 was largely a consequence of the expansionary financing of the defense program. The relative weight of the nonexpansionary sources of financing should not be underestimated. Fiscal revenues rose by roughly 40 per cent, and nondefense outlays of the federal government declined by about 10 per cent. These two sources contributed nearly 3 billions to Treasury finance. Furthermore, about one-third of the borrowing of the Treasury and the agencies was from lenders other than banks. This nonexpansionary borrowing accounted for almost 2 billions, whereas in the previous year it had not accounted for more than about 600 millions. In spite of this, the expansionary gap was wide enough to raise the annual rate of new-money creation to about 7.5 billions. The substantial rise in the loans and investments of the banks was largely a direct consequence of government borrowing from the banking system. Government borrowing from banks accounts for roughly half the new money and for the entire rise in the investments of banks. The increase in bank loans also was largely an immediate consequence of defense activities.

We have also seen that until about February, 1941, the increased supply of money did not raise prices substantially. From the beginning of the fiscal year up to February the rise in wholesale prices was less than 4 per cent and the rise in the cost of living was less than 1 per cent. After February the rise in the price level became substantial. It might therefore be said that until early in 1941 the monetary expansion *per se* did not produce significant effects of an undesirable kind. We could argue that the new money was allowed partly to flow into channels in which it stimulated an undesirable rise in the output of consumers' goods. But a widening of the money flow was necessary, since otherwise a pressure on the price level would have stood in the way of the rise in real output. Since the early part of 1941, however, the rate of new-money creation is clearly in excess of what is required to avoid a pressure on prices. At that time the failure to raise a sufficiently high proportion of the defense funds by nonexpansionary methods began to lead to a distinctly undesirable upward movement of the price structure.

The early part of the third fiscal year.—In the first five to six months of the fiscal year 1942—that is, prior to the attack on Pearl Harbor—the rate of new-money creation seemed to remain approximately unchanged. Before war was declared, the national defense expenditures of the federal government were estimated at 18 billions for fiscal 1942, and total federal expenditures were expected to reach about 24 billions. With revenues estimated at 12 billions a crude deficit of roughly 12 billions seemed probable. The defense expenditures of the R.F.C. and its subsidiaries were also on the increase. Both the crude and the corrected deficit would have amounted to two to three times (presumably closer to three) the level of the preceding fiscal year, even if merely the plans of the last prebelligerent stage were being carried out. This was the situation in spite of the fact that income-tax rates as well as excise taxes were substantially increased in the early part of the fiscal year.

On the other hand, there was also an increase in security sales to the public,[10] so that in the last stage prior to the war

---

[10] In the first six months of the fiscal year slightly over 4 billions in defense bonds and tax anticipation notes were sold to buyers other than banks. The

declarations the expansionary gap of fiscal 1942 seemed to be of the same order of magnitude as that of the preceding fiscal year. The rise in bank loans also continued at a roughly unchanging rate, while the gold influx slowed down appreciably. It seemed likely that the supply of money would increase at approximately the same rate as in the fiscal year 1941. Nevertheless, the danger of inflation did become more acute. This is a consequence of the slowing down of "real" expansion. As has been pointed out above, the rate of increase of real output has become much smaller since the beginning of the fiscal year under consideration. The same increase in the supply of money obviously gives rise to a smaller inflationary pressure if it is accompanied by a substantial increase in real output. This is the reason why the danger of inflation seemed imminent prior to December 7.

The full economic impact of the actual participation of the United States in the war will not be felt until the fiscal year 1943, but since Pearl Harbor the estimates of defense expenditures have been revised significantly upward, even for fiscal 1942. Defense spending for the fiscal year 1942 will amount to about 26 billions (instead of the 18 billions previously estimated), and aggregate federal expenditures to about 32 billions (instead of 24 billions). Net receipts for fiscal 1942 will apparently not exceed the previously estimated 12 to 13 billions and consequently the estimated deficit rose by about 8 billions (to almost 20 billions). These revisions mean a higher rate of monetary expansion, and also a higher rate of output curtailment in the civilian sector.

The behavior of velocity.—War finance becomes inflationary not merely if it leads to a rise in the stock of money, but

---

average sales of these six months were already slightly influenced by the reaction to Pearl Harbor and to the subsequent events. Yet statistics relating to somewhat shorter periods within the first half of fiscal 1942 also lead to the conclusion that sales of the bonds and notes were at an annual rate of roughly 8 billions. Including the borrowing from insurance companies, the amount of 8 billions would probably have been slightly exceeded.

also if it causes the velocity of money to increase. Generally speaking, there is a strong presumption that taxation and borrowing from the public are less expansionary than is borrowing from banks, since both taxation and borrowing from the public may be assumed to cut down other expenditures. Yet the other expenditures of the public are not necessarily curtailed by the full amount of lendings and of tax payments, and hence a rise in the effective circulation is not necessarily avoided by these methods. This is partly because the buyer of government securities or the taxpayer may increase his borrowings from the banking system. The stock of money then rises just as if the government were borrowing from banks. The potentiality of expansionary effects, however, is partly a consequence of the fact that the taxpayer or the buyer of government securities may deplete his idle cash balances.[11] The velocity of money—its exchange velocity as well as its income velocity—then tends to rise.

The attempt to decrease the amount of cash balances held per unit of expenditure may be a direct reaction to the burden involved in taxpaying and in lending to the government. The public is forced to pay taxes and may feel a strong impulse to buy government securities, but it may prefer to decrease its liquid assets rather than curtail its expenditures by the full equivalent. As the taxpayer sees it, if taxes are paid by depleting idle funds, capital consumption occurs, whereas lending idle funds to the government merely implies the exchange of one type of assets (cash) against another type (government bonds). Hence the likelihood of payments out of hoards, as against payment out of current income, is greater for borrowing than for taxation. Yet the tendency to deplete idle balances may also be a consequence of inflationary expectations rather than of consumers' resistance to the lowering of the standard of living. If prices are expected to rise and the value of the

---

[11] Or he may sell securities to other members of the "public" who deplete their cash balances.

The Financing of Defense

money to decline, preferences are shifted away from money toward real assets.

In time of war all these considerations acquire significance. It is a fact, however, that no important change in velocity was noticeable even in the period preceding the O.P.A. regulations. Table 3 shows the income velocity of the dollar for the years 1939, 1940, and 1941. The changes are so small that, considering the limitations of estimates like these, we have to conclude

TABLE 3
INCOME VELOCITY CALCULATED FROM ALTERNATIVE INCOME CONCEPTS

Income concept	1939	1940	1941
Income payments..................	1.97	1.84	1.84
National income at factor costs......	1.97	1.87	1.94
National income at market prices....	2.23	2.13	2.26

All income estimates are those of the U. S. Department of Commerce. As to the stock of money, cf. table 9 in the Appendix.

that income velocity remained approximately unchanged during this two-year period. It can also be seen from the table that the figures are little affected by the choice of the income concept the ratio of which to the stock of money is defined as income velocity. The figures of the table are calculated from aggregate income payments, from national income at factor costs, and from national income at market prices.

As a concept, exchange velocity is more closely related to trends in hoarding than is income velocity. Nevertheless, it is questionable whether the currently published exchange-velocity indexes are superior measures of changes in the hoarding ratio. The reason is that exchange velocity indexes relate merely to the turnover of bank deposits. No current estimates are available for the rate of turnover of hand-to-hand currency. As against this, hand-to-hand currency is included in the stock of money when income velocity is derived; and trends in income velocity are unlikely to be very different from trends in exchange velocity.

Chart 6 shows the behavior of the exchange velocity of bank deposits for the period. The chart is based on estimates of the Federal Reserve Bank of New York, which in turn are derived from the amount of bank deposits and bank debits. The behavior of this exchange-velocity index can best be characterized

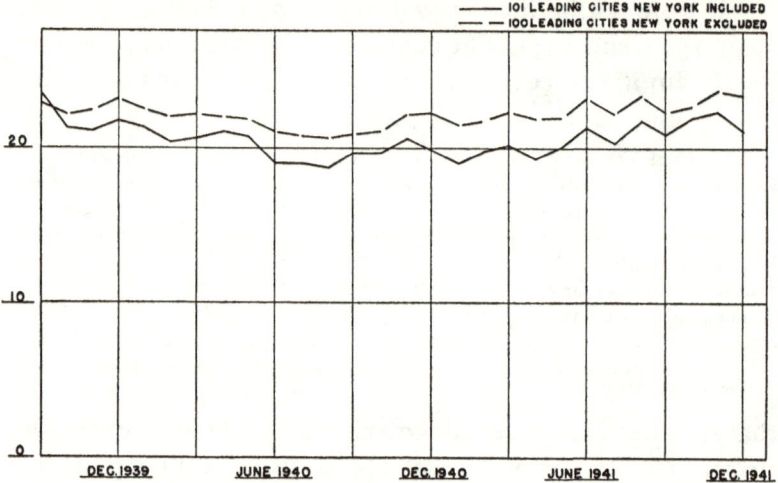

Chart 6. Exchange velocity of bank deposits, September, 1939–December, 1941.
SOURCE: "Annual Rate of Turnover of Demand Deposits, Federal Reserve Bank of New York, Revision of 1941, Adjusted for Seasonal Variations" (mim.).

by the statement that there was first a small decline which later was almost offset by a slight rise. Recently the exchange-velocity figures have been approximately at their prewar levels.

It should be emphasized that roughly unchanging velocity in the given circumstances does not mean a roughly unchanging absolute amount of idle deposits. In 1939, idle deposits undoubtedly were at a high level. Professor Angell has shown that the income velocity of the dollar, for example, remained substantially below its predepression level throughout the 1930's.[12] His estimates indicate that income velocity, which prior to the great depression used to fluctuate near a level of 3, has not in 1939 exceeded the level of 2. Exchange velocity,

[12] James W. Angell, *Investment and Business Cycles* (New York, McGraw-Hill, 1941), chap. ix and App. ii.

The Financing of Defense

too, shows a sharply declining trend from the 1920's to the 1930's.[13] This substantial decline in velocity figures undoubtedly reflects a high amount of idle deposits. The behavior of velocity since the outbreak of the war in Europe indicates that recently idle balances must have increased further.

From the summer of 1939 to the summer of 1941 the stock of money rose by about one-third. The addition to the money stock in the course of these two years amounts to roughly 12 billions.[14] The fact that velocity has not risen indicates that the addition to the supply of money must have been divided into active money and idle balances in roughly the same proportion as the 1939 stock. It may even be assumed that idle balances have risen in a slightly higher proportion than active balances, since it is likely that the velocity of the active-money balances—that is, of the so-called working balances—has increased somewhat. It seems that there was, and is, a tendency to tighten the terms of payment, which in turn tends to raise the velocity of the working balances. With no change in the velocity of working balances, an unchanging average velocity of the dollar would indicate that idle balances and working balances rose in the same proportion. In the event of a rise in the velocity of the working balances, unchanging average velocity points to a more than proportionate increase in idle money.

Even if we should assume that the two types of cash balances rose in the same proportion, the rise in the absolute amount of idle money would seem to be very significant. Even on this assumption, we should have to conclude that the significant

---

[13] Exchange velocity of 101 cities, including New York, was as follows:

Year	Value	Year	Value
1926	55.1	1933	32.6
1927	59.7	1934	30.9
1928	70.3	1935	29.7
1929	80.1	1936	29.6
1930	56.9	1937	28.8
1931	42.7	1938	24.9
1932	33.6	1939	22.5

SOURCE: Federal Reserve Bank of New York.

[14] See table 9, Appendix.

amount of idle balances existing in 1939 has, up to the summer of 1941, risen by about one third. This seems to have happened even when business activity was expanding at a rapid rate and the continuation of the upward trend in business activity and in prices was expected. It is true, of course, that the degree of definiteness with which the public believed that it could foresee the future was small. An early collapse of the boom did not seem probable to many people, but a collapse of the expansion was a possibility which had to be taken into account in business dispositions. Furthermore, the obvious potentiality of government regulations as affecting the profitability of real investments may also have provided an inducement to hoard. Hence, investment activity rose substantially; but at the same time, idle balances also rose by a considerable margin. The real expansion reflects, in a sense, an optimistic evaluation of future business developments. The rise in idle balances reflects a desire to provide for contingencies. The expectations of the public are not "single-valued": the attempt to take account of different possibilities may lead to apparently paradoxical behavior.

If in the future a tendency to deplete idle balances should become prevalent, inflationary phenomena would thereby be strongly accentuated. A rise of the income velocity of the present stock of money to the velocity level of the 1920's would, of itself, raise the annual rate of money income by more than 60 billions.

CHAPTER V

Noninflationary War Finance

● *Could inflation tendencies be completely avoided in a major war?*—This chapter contains an inquiry into the possibilities of noninflationary war finance without taking into account difficulties usually designated as *political*. In other words, the problem will be discussed in terms of economic analysis in the narrower sense. Conclusions to be derived from so narrow an approach are not significant *per se,* but methodologically it seems convenient to isolate different aspects of one and the same problem. In the next chapter the analysis will be extended to aspects other than the strictly "economic" ones.

The possibility of completely noninflationary war finance should not be taken for granted even in a narrow technical approach. Even if all legislation considered sound by economists could be enacted without delay, and there were no question of undesirable political repercussions, the public in a major war might still tend to generate phenomena of an inflationary sort. It is unlikely, however, that in such circumstances the inflation tendency would become substantial.

A politically omnipotent government[1] might, in the attempt to forestall inflation, completely avoid borrowing from banks. So long as total physical production is rising, such a policy would seem unjustified; but the point is that borrowing from banks could be kept at any level which seemed desirable, including the zero level. Furthermore, the public could also be prevented from increasing its bank debts whenever this should seem desirable to the monetary authority. A ceiling on the stock of money is, in principle, simply a matter of reserve re-

---
[1] No real government is "omnipotent" in this sense. Totalitarian governments may have to pay even more attention to the conditions of equilibrium between internal groups than democratic governments do.

quirements. Banks are in no position to increase their loans and investments if whatever reserve balances they have are classified as required reserves and if the central banking system prevents the formation of new reserve balances. A politically omnipotent government could acquire all funds necessary for the conduct of a war by means of taxation or compulsory lending, and could also prevent the banks from increasing their loans to the public.

Yet no government could be certain of preventing a rise in the velocity of money simply by controlling the credit mechanism. It would always be possible for the public to pay taxes or purchase government securities by decreasing its idle-money balances. As taxpaying, this would imply, from the taxpayers' standpoint, capital consumption, and undoubtedly there is a resistance against meeting burdens by consuming assets. The degree of taxation which would be required to finance a major war without resorting to loans of any kind would be so high, however, that the public might not meet the entire tax burden by reducing its current expenditures. Assuming a progressive tax structure which hits present savers and potential dissavers hard, there is even a strong presumption that some part of the tax payments would tend to come out of funds previously idle. If taxation and borrowing from the public were to be combined, but borrowing from banks were to be excluded, the tendency to deplete idle balances would be even more marked, since the resistance against investing idle funds in government securities is smaller than the resistance against consuming assets under the pressure of the tax burden.

The tendency of velocity to rise would itself justify certain direct controls, such as the rationing of consumers' goods combined with price control, even if "inflationary borrowing" could be completely avoided. The controls could, of course, prevent the dishoarding which would occur on free markets. If their scope and effectiveness were great enough they could even enforce a substantial amount of net new saving and of net new hoarding. Yet such savings as are enforced by direct consumers' controls cannot be regarded as a source of noninflationary war finance. To the extent of these savings the inflation tendency is, for the time being, effectively controlled, but it has not been annihilated. The avoidance of inflation tendencies would imply that no controls would be required to prevent the general price level from rising. The only function of direct controls in a noninflationary war-finance policy would be that of directing demand away from certain commodities toward others.

No fiscal policy will alone suppress reliably all inflation tendencies in a war requiring roughly half the output flow. This would be true even if we could disregard those factors which thus far have consistently required governments to borrow from banks. Yet the main inflationary effect of great wars is a consequence of direct borrowing operations from the banking system. These borrowing operations cannot be satisfactorily explained in terms of economics alone. Hence it seems reasonable to divide our problem into two parts. We shall assume here that the government is free to tax at all rates appearing justified on purely rational grounds. On this assumption it is possible to outline a tax policy which would approximate the ideal of noninflationary war finance rather closely—although, for reasons indicated above, inflation tendencies could not be ruled out entirely. In the subsequent chapter the question will be raised why tax policies of this character are not adopted in reality, and various types of compromises between different points of view will be compared.

The general case for income taxes.—The taxation of income represents the most equitable method of distributing the burden of a war. This is true because income taxes can be so applied as to make the financial status of the taxpayer one of the determinants of the burden imposed upon him. It is commonly considered desirable to tax the more well-to-do sections of the population at a higher rate than those less well off. This clearly calls for income taxation, so far as we accept the size of income as a measure of how well off a person is in relation to others. The size of income is not an unequivocal measure of economic well-being, but income may be considered the most significant single determinant of well-being in the economic sense. Consequently, a progressive income-tax scale which, aside from the size of incomes, takes account of other factors such as size of families and capital gains and losses is more nearly capable of conforming with prevailing preferences than other methods of taxation. How far other criteria should be combined with the size-of-income criterion remains a matter of individual judgment, and no consensus should be presupposed in this respect; yet, once income is accorded the role of the most important single determinant of economic well-being, it becomes appropriate to take account of other determinants in the framework of an income-tax mechanism rather than allow for the size of income in the framework of a tax mechanism based on other criteria.

The reasons for the common acceptance of the desirability of progressive taxation need not be discussed here at great length. The reader's attention may, however, be directed to a specific circumstance in this connection. A progressive tax, as opposed to linear taxes, changes the net position of the different income recipients in relation to one another. If A can buy twice as many commodities for his income as B, then the 2:1 relationship will still apply to the situation as modified by a linear tax; but the relationship will have shifted against A, that is, in favor of B, if a progressive tax is applied. Now, one of the justifications of progressiveness is that public opinion in the democratic countries is favorably inclined toward equalitarian measures in general. It is important to realize, however, that the sentiment for wartime progressiveness does not rest exclusively on these general considerations. Some of the marked inequalities are considered justified in normal times, since the services of some of the high-income recipients are felt to be worth a multiple of the services of average men. Not all the high-grade service could be obtained for low rewards; and, aside from this, the curtailment of the reward would frequently not even seem fair to most people. In times of total war the attitude toward this problem is apt to change, however. This is a consequence of two peculiarities of a war economics. First, the significance of the acquisitive motive, as of a necessary incentive to efficiency, is reduced. Defeat is so extremely costly to every member of a community that intelligent people must be assumed to have strong incentives other than the income motive tending to stimulate them to high performances. Second, as a matter of equity, it may be felt that group A should earn several times as much as group B if group B has enough to maintain some accepted minimum standard, but that the ratio should be reduced before group B is forced to descend substantially below that standard. This latter view acquires high significance in total war. As will be seen later, high progressiveness in a war like the present one would have to be largely at the expense of the so-called middle-income brackets. In normal times there is not much sentiment against the rather substantial degree of inequality reflecting itself in the earnings of these groups; yet it is generally felt that equity demands the imposition of a much higher than average burden on these groups before the lowest income groups are pressed far below their peacetime level.

For the most part, the problem of the "appropriate" degree of progressiveness lies, of course, outside the scope of rationality. Obviously, however, high progression would be imposed by logical necessity upon a noninflationary war-finance policy if that policy should rely exclusively on income taxes and retain the principle of exemptions for the lowest income groups. The discussion in the present chapter rests on the assumption that it is not necessary to combine income taxes with other types of taxation merely to diminish progressiveness. In other words, it will be assumed that the rational policy under consideration interprets numerous expressions of public opinion to indicate that progressiveness *per se* should be considered an advantage rather than a disadvantage. This means that, for the policy assumed, proposals to raise certain parts of the war fund by methods other than income taxation require specific justification, and that the justification must not imply that high progression is a disadvantage or that political difficulties prevent the government from adopting the measures best suited. We shall now turn to the circumstance which, even in the framework of such a policy, would justify the combination of other methods with income taxation. The problem will be discussed with reference to the present situation of the American war economy. Later, certain phenomena will be discussed which, on realistic assumptions regarding the behavior of social communities, favor heavier reliance on consumption taxes than that which appears justified on the present assumptions.

Expansionary financing.—The required increase in the money flow may be brought about by different amounts of new money, depending on what the velocity of the money stock turns out to be. The assumption of constant velocity—an assumption which is to be made on subsequent pages—implies that individual dishoarding, which would raise consumption expenditures, is prevented by the controls and that new corporate hoarding is prevented by effective borrowing campaigns. The qualifications will be considered later.

In chapter iii we have argued that in the United States a rise of real output in excess of 20 per cent for the next two years is improbable. This would correspond to an average annual rate of real growth not exceeding 10 per cent. For a longer period the average annual rate of real expansion would, very likely, be even smaller. Hence a policy excluding all theoretically avoidable inflationary effects would not let money incomes rise at an annual rate of more than about 10 per cent. In later stages of the war, 10 per cent may even be too high. Considering that the stock of money is now somewhat in excess of 50 billions, this would mean that borrowing from banks at an annual rate of about 5 to 6 billions seems justified, assuming that the rise in real output contemplated above will be realized.

In this connection, reference should be made to the previous discussion of the difference existing between expansionary effects in general and induced consumption and investment effects in particular. Expansionary effects should be allowed within narrow limits, but even the small amount of monetary expansion which can be justified in these circumstances should not be allowed to express itself in induced private expenditures. The fiscal policy appropriate to this objective is that of increasing the tax liabilities of individuals by the amount by which their expenditures should be curtailed plus the full amount of the rise in their money incomes.[2]

The question also arises how the present method of selling securities to member banks compares with direct borrowing from the Federal Reserve banks. On purely rational grounds it might be concluded that eliminating the present legal limits to direct borrowing from the Federal Reserve would have advantages over security sales to member banks. It may well be, however, that irrational factors turn the balance in the opposite direction.

Borrowing from the Federal Reserve banks might render it possible to eliminate the existing excess reserves of the member banks. At present the excess reserves cannot be eliminated, because this would impair the borrowing operations of the Treasury; and even if security sales to member banks were reduced to a rate corresponding to the growth of physical output, it still would be necessary to leave the banks with reserves in excess of legal requirements. This has the disadvantage that the banks are in a position to increase their lendings to indi-

---

[2] This is the reason why the appropriate degree of monetary expansion could not be brought about by leaving the potential tendency to dishoard uncontrolled instead of by undertaking some amount of expansionary borrowing. The tendency to dishoard is a tendency to raise private expenditures.

viduals and to institutions other than the federal government. A door is left open for loans and investments with no assurance that the Treasury will be the only institution to use the door. New bank loans not serving the objectives of war finance could be forestalled, if all lending for war purposes should be undertaken by the Federal Reserve banks and the reserve requirements for the rest of the banking system should be so changed as to keep excess reserves at the zero level.

A policy aiming at this objective would, of course, have to prevent the formation of new excess reserves once the excess should be eliminated as of a certain date. This does not merely mean that the Federal Reserve banks would have to refrain from rediscounting bills and, generally speaking, from the purchase of all securities other than newly issued securities of the federal government. A more difficult problem is involved in such a policy. The spending of Treasury funds originally borrowed from the Federal Reserve banks automatically leads to the formation of new excess reserves, since in the course of this process individuals (in the first instance, producers of war materials and of war services) acquire deposits in commercial banks and the commercial banks acquire deposits of identical size in their Federal Reserve Banks. A policy attempting to keep the banks "loaned up" continuously would have to take care of this difficulty in some fashion. The difficulty, however, is a technical one. In principle, the newly formed excess reserves could be absorbed by a continuous adjustment of reserve requirements; yet such a procedure might prove rather inexpedient in practice. The most expedient solution might be to require 100 per cent reserve for all future rise in deposits. If reserve requirements should be so changed as to wipe out excess reserves as of a certain date and 100 per cent reserve should be required for any addition to the existing stock of bank deposits, then the Treasury could borrow from the Federal Reserve banks without thereby creating a lending potential for other purposes.

On rational grounds such an arrangement would seem preferable to the method of borrowing from the member banks. The reform could well be recommended to a hypothetical government aiming at complete avoidance of inflationary phenomena, especially if the assumption were made that no amount of political pressure could induce our hypothetical government to undertake expansionary borrowing in excess of the rate of physical growth.

The analysis would become less conclusive if political circumstances should be taken into account. As soon as the degree of inflationary borrowing is conceived as depending on the ease of such borrowing, a further consideration enters. The possibility of direct borrowing from the central banks makes it easy for governments to carry out inflationary borrowing operations. Would such a possibility not weaken their incentive to tax? Would it not increase the political pressure toward lenient taxation? Should this be the result, then it might be preferable to keep this channel blocked, in spite of the fact that borrowing from the member banks presupposes the existence of excess reserves and consequently implies some danger of secondary inflationary effects.

On realistic assumptions it is difficult to form a conclusive opinion in this matter. The dangers implied in direct borrowing are frequently overestimated. The federal government will presumably not have serious difficulties in borrowing whatever it wishes to borrow from the member banks. Once the government has the assistance of the Federal Reserve Board, reserve requirements can always be so lowered and central banking policies so handled as to maintain the market for government securities even if direct borrowing from the Federal Reserve banks is prohibited or limited to insignificant amounts. This consideration would provide an argument in favor of direct borrowing. Yet, it still may be true that there is some difference between the "ease" of direct borrowing and the "ease" of security sales to the member banks. So far as there is such a difference, the misgivings about legislation permitting direct borrowing may not be entirely unfounded. Moreover, the government might have means by which the member banks could be prevented from embarking on "undesirable" expansion even if they should be left with excess reserves. Hence, on realistic assumptions it is not obvious which of these two methods is preferable to the other; the difference may not be very great.

Excises.—Financing by methods other than income taxation seems justified not merely to the extent to which expansionary borrowing should be continued. The principle that progressive taxes are preferable to others is subject to the qualification that the taxation of luxuries and of harmful commodities may perform a socially desirable function. The notion of the "appropriate degree" of such taxation is, of course, more than vague. When the raising of fiscal revenue by taxing such commodities as liquor and tobacco is considered desirable, the implication essentially is that a wise government, or a wise community, is better able to judge the true interests of the individual than is the individual himself. Implicit in this argument is the same distinction as that drawn by Pareto, who contrasted the concept of *utility* (meaning the true utility of a commodity) with the concept of *ophelimity* (mere desirability). Income taxation rests on the notion that the tax system should discriminate in favor of the lower income brackets, regardless of what they consume. The American excise structure may be interpreted to rest largely, although not entirely, on the notion that taxation should discriminate against the consumers of mere "ophelimities." The criteria of true utility being indistinct, all analysis resting on the difference between these two concepts must necessarily lack definiteness. By distinguishing "utility" from "ophelimity" one may conclude that a slight deterrent to unreasonable spending is in order, or one may go so far as to advocate national prohibition. The optimum point cannot be calculated on definite criteria.

It is a fact, however, that the federal government, in the fiscal year 1941, collected about 2.4 billions from excises; and the revenue to be raised from this source in fiscal 1942 might add up to somewhat more than 3 billions. The rise is mainly a consequence of increases in tax rates which became effective in October, 1941. Early in March, 1942, the Treasury submitted to Congress tax proposals which would add another 1.3 billions to the excise tax revenue. About one-half of this rise and more than one-half of the expected total revenue would be contributed by alcoholic beverages and by tobacco products. Few people feel that excise taxation at the level now contemplated, or even at a somewhat higher level, would produce socially undesirable consequences. If income taxes were to be increased severely, some further increase in excise taxation would generally be considered justified.

It must not, however, be overlooked that the consumption of some of the taxed items is bound to decline. This is not mainly a consequence of the price-elasticity of demand. A revenue of roughly 6 to 7 billions could probably be attained with no great difficulty, in spite of the fact that higher prices would tend to reduce consumption. Yet some of the taxed items of consumption, such as durable consumers' goods and gasoline, are competing directly with war production and hence the allocation of resources to war industries weakens certain constituents of the excise structure. This might tend to reduce the excise revenue between 15 and 20 per cent.

The scarcity which will arise in some fields may, however, justify the application of high excise rates. Tax rates of such magnitude as could not easily be justified merely by the foregoing considerations may become appropriate in fields of high scarcity. In practice, no level of income taxation would of itself prevent the prices of highly scarce commodities from rising. Even should half the national output be allocated to the war and taxation be increased to a level high enough to keep the general price level approximately stable, there would still be a strong tendency for the prices of highly scarce commodities to rise, since the supply of these commodities would be curtailed in a much higher than average proportion. We have seen earlier that this consideration would justify some degree of rationing and of price control even if an upward pressure on the general price level could be avoided. But it does not follow that an attempt should be made to keep the prices of highly scarce commodities in relation to other prices at the level at which they happened to be when the commodities in question were abundant. It does not seem possible to exclude relative price movements entirely from the process of limiting the demand for highly scarce goods. The upward pressure on the prices of these commodities would be so high at practically all levels of income taxation as to render the effectiveness of the controls incomplete. Moreover, in some fields of high scarcity the relative significance of secondhand markets is bound to increase; and to enforce direct controls on these markets is especially difficult. Hence, whether we like it or not, the mechanism of relative price movements will become one of the rationing factors. Now, it is obviously preferable to utilize the inevitable rise in certain prices for the purposes of war finance rather than allow these price movements to create substantial windfall profits. This justifies increased excise taxation in the fields of high scarcity, on secondhand as well as on new markets. The price, including tax, would then rise, but price fixing, combined with rationing, would be much more effective at the increased levels, where the excess of demand over supply is correspondingly smaller. It infrequently happens that the scarcity arises in a commodity which may reasonably be classified as a "basic necessary"; an effort should then be made to keep prices at a roughly unchanging level, regardless of the monetary pressure to be overcome. Shortages in sugar and low-priced clothing or footwear are examples. It does not follow, however, that relative price movements could or should be excluded from the "rationing" process throughout, and it is preferable to bring forth certain shifts within the price structure by the means of excise taxation rather than allow these shifts to result in profiteering.

We have assumed previously that at the present income level an annual yield of about 6 to 7 billions could be obtained by excise taxation, somewhat higher than is now contemplated, unless the future scarcity of taxed commodities upsets this calculation. Considering, however, the possibility of using excises as a means of diverting demand from fields of high scarcity, the estimate need not be revised downward.

Borrowing from voluntary savings; corporate income taxes.— To the extent to which the government may borrow from the current stream of net savings—that is, "out of current income"—borrowing may be substituted for taxation without inflationary consequences. In spite of this, borrowing out of savings as a substitute for taxation requires specific justification since it results in a different distribution of burdens. The buyer of a government security acquires a claim against the community as a whole; the taxpayer does not. This point is all the more worth emphasizing because normally persons in the higher income brackets save a larger portion of their incomes than those in the lower. Hence reliance on borrowing from the stream of voluntary savings rather than on taxation results, on balance, in the acquisition of claims by the relatively well-to-do against the lower brackets, within the "universe" of taxpayers. Moreover, a transfer is created with potentially adverse effects on the general level of output in the postwar economy.

Given the burden occasioned by the present war, this well-known dilemma would presumably not arise with respect to borrowing from individual savings if the government should confine itself to noninflationary methods of war finance. As was pointed out, the savings indirectly enforced by the means of consumers' controls—rationing and price control—should be disregarded in discussions of the sources of noninflationary war finance. Avoiding the inflation tendency means avoiding these savings which result from redundant incomes and represent suppressed inflationary purchasing power. The genuine tendency to save would be slight in a period in which real consumption income must be lowered substantially. Consequently, a policy attempting to raise almost the entire war fund by taxation plus borrowing from genuine savings would have to rely mainly on taxation, and by so doing would reduce the small amount of genuine individual savings even further, unless the tax structure were distinctly regressive.

It does not follow, however, that all noninflationary borrowing would have to cease. Borrowing from business savings might retain some significance so long as corporate taxes should not become entirely confiscatory. The relationship between individual taxation and individual saving is different from that between corporate taxation and corporate saving. High rates of personal taxation reduce or eliminate individual saving. Yet high rates of individual taxation coupled with high rates of corporate taxation do not necessarily eliminate corporate saving. On the contrary, there is a strong incentive not to distribute an unnecessarily large share of corporate earnings in the form of dividend payments so long as these are subject to individual income taxation at wartime rates. Moreover, the tendency to retain corporate earnings should be strengthened rather than counteracted by government policy, since counteracting this tendency is tantamount to stimulating consumption expenditures. Limitation of dividend payments seems to be an appropriate wartime measure. If such a policy were pursued, borrowing from net corporate earnings might amount to several billions per year.

The alternative policy with respect to corporations is, of course, to make corporate income taxes almost confiscatory— in which event corporate saving would obviously shrink almost to nothing. Such a policy would do more harm than good. To exclude the profit stimulus entirely is risky when maximum efficiency of business enterprise is vital for victory. It is not to be denied that in times of war there are important stimuli to increased efficiency besides the profit motive, but to exclude the profit stimulus completely means taking chances. It is desirable therefore to keep marginal corporate income tax rates far enough below 100 per cent to provide an effective profit incentive. This obviously has implications with respect to average tax rates, since, with taxes progressive, average rates must fall short of marginal rates. If business taxation remains within limits determined by this consideration, and if a substantial portion of the earnings after taxes is taken up by government borrowing, then, of course, to this extent the war creates claims in favor of corporations against the community. This is not a desirable objective in itself; in consideration of the quantitative aspects of the problem, however, it seems well worth while to leave some of the profit stimulus.

It seems likely that the Treasury proposals submitted to Congress in March, 1942, would have resulted in taxing away about 60 per cent of the corporate earnings. The proposed top rates were 55 per cent for normal profits in excess of $25,000 and 75 per cent for excess profits of more than $500,000. The Treasury apparently expected that these rates—which, however, will not be passed without modifications—would yield around 10 billions in the fiscal year 1943. If this corresponds roughly to 60 per cent, then the remaining corporate earnings after taxes could not have amounted to much more than about 7 billions; possibly they would even have amounted to somewhat less.[3] Corporate taxation corresponding to the Treasury proposals of March, 1942, together with a limitation of dividend payments to 50 per cent of the remaining net earnings, might therefore render it possible to raise, by the means of corporate taxation plus borrowing from profits, a yearly fund of about 13 to 14 billions. Such a settlement would create

---

[3] The proportionate increase in profits since 1939 has been very high, however. According to the Department of Commerce, corporate earnings after taxes amounted to 4.2 billions in 1939, 5.5 billions in 1940, and 7.2 billions in 1941. The proportionate increase would be even more substantial if profits before taxes were compared for these three years. See *Bulletin No. 1* of the Office of Price Administration.

claims in favor of corporations at an annual rate of only about 3 to 4 billions.

Whether the war lending of corporations has to be called "voluntary" or "forced" is largely a matter of terminology. The lack of other investment opportunities would probably induce enterprises to make a large share of their savings available for the purposes of war finance. Moreover, as we have noted earlier, high individual tax rates tend to increase the rate of corporate saving. War loans induced by the interaction of merely these two circumstances, would presumably be called "voluntary," in spite of the fact that the range of alternatives among which business enterprises can choose is strongly reduced as compared with the range under normal conditions. If, in addition, dividend payments are limited, "compulsion" is more closely approached, but there still remains a choice between lending for war finance and hoarding. In reality, the limitation of dividend payments would presumably direct a large share of the corporate savings into the market for government securities or into direct war investment, especially if tax rates were fixed so as to discriminate against the allocation of undistributed profits to other uses. But compulsory lending in the narrower, legal sense might also be considered.

Borrowing from depreciation and liquidation funds.—Undistributed net profits are not the only business funds which would become available for the purposes of noninflationary war finance. The undermaintenance of plant and equipment and the depletion of inventories in the civilian sector will also lead to the accumulation of such funds as are part of the gross savings of the economy. So far as private war investment does not offset this capital consumption, the government may borrow and spend the corresponding amounts without thereby producing inflationary effects. In chapter iii we have estimated that capital consumption in the civilian sector may for some time run at an annual rate of about 8 billions, and that the excess of capital consumption over private war investment may reach a rate of about 5 billions. This excess is part of the gross business savings from which the government could borrow without inflationary consequences. In a longer-run analysis we would have to take account of the fact that deferring replacements may result in a postponed inflationary effect.

Should the savings be borrowed, or should saving merely offset borrowing?—In the preceding pages a terminology was used which will now be *qualified* slightly, but mainly *justified*. We spoke of borrowing from savings and concluded that, in the framework of noninflationary war finance, borrowing from individual savings could not acquire significance, while borrowing from gross business savings might conceivably correspond to about 8 billions per year, out of which roughly 3 billions might be from net business savings. The question arises whether we should not preferably say that on these numerical assumptons the government might borrow 8 billions annually from whomever it chooses, including banks, so long as the savers of this amount are effectively prevented from investing their savings and from lending it for nonessential expenditures.

It is quite true that borrowing operations from the public or from the banks will not result in any simultaneous rise in money income so long as some individual or institution saves the corresponding amount out of current income and fails to invest it. Nevertheless, it is preferable to borrow so far as possible from savers rather than to have hoarding by savers offset the borrowing from other sources. The latter procedure leads to the accumulation of idle deposits which may tend to become active in a later stage of the war or in the immediate postwar short run. The future monetary controls will be more nearly effective if an abnormally high degree of liquidity is avoided. Consequently, it is preferable to borrow "out of the current flow of savings" in a more literal rather than in a purely aggregative sense. This objective can, of course, never be achieved completely, but it may be possible to concentrate mainly on borrowing from those potential lenders who, in the circumstances, may be assumed to accumulate savings.

Compulsory individual saving.—Thus far we have discussed sources of war finance other than individual income taxation, which, at the income level to be expected in the fiscal year 1943, might yield a revenue of about 30 to 32 billions. Since in the fiscal year 1943 the expenditures of the Treasury are expected to exceed 70 billions, an amount of about 40 billions would remain to be raised by personal income taxation.[4] There are two reasons, however, why compulsory lending might be combined with taxation proper to raise this fund.

First, as has been pointed out by Lord Keynes, the combination of compulsory lending with taxation might serve the purpose of rendering the long-term distribution of burdens more favorable for the low-income classes. It is necessary to impose, during the war, a substantial burden on all groups of the population. This does not in itself limit the tax rate which may be applied to the high-income brackets, but it requires the application of rather high rates to rather low incomes even if very high rates are applied to the middle brackets and especially to the high-income groups. Now, obviously, one way of making the long-term distribution of burdens more advantageous for the low-income brackets is to create claims in their favor against the community as a whole.

If, for example, Social Security contributions are increased and the federal government borrows the yield of the increased payroll taxes from the Social Security system, then, in a sense, compulsory lending for the purposes of war finance may be said to take place. The members of the Social Security system are expected to get these "advances" refunded in the form of postwar benefits, even if no commitment is made with respect to time and specific character of the benefit. Other types of postwar credit imply more specific commitments.

---

[4] Other sources of revenue, here not considered, yield negligible amounts as compared with the orders of magnitude involved in the present problem.

Aside from this, the method of compulsory loans may also be used to keep marginal tax rates far enough below 100 per cent to provide an effective stimulus to increased effort. An income-tax scale yielding a high proportion of national income must necessarily become steeply progressive if the lowest income brackets are to be exempted. The marginal rate must, of course, be consistently kept below 100 per cent, and consequently average rates must be low in the immediate neighborhood of the exemption limit. Yet, since marginal rates exceed average rates for the various brackets, and since high average rates must be applied to the middle brackets and especially to high-income groups, heavy reliance on income taxation renders it necessary to approximate a marginal rate of 100 per cent in the upper section of the scale. But by combining compulsory lending with taxation it is possible to avoid marginal rates of such height. For that portion of tax liabilities which corresponds to a marginal rate of more than, say, 80 per cent a compulsory loan might be substituted.

It should not, however, be overlooked that all types of compulsory loans have the drawback of leaving a bill to be settled in the postwar period. Advocates of compulsory lending schemes usually point out that settling the bill may have beneficial effects at the time of the settlement. In a postwar depression the repayment of loans to the low-income brackets may, for example, contribute to the maintenance of consumption expenditures. Whether a stimulus would be created by repayments if the necessary funds should be acquired by the taxation of the high-income brackets or by a capital levy is questionable, since the potential adverse effects of these taxes cannot be disregarded. If, on the other hand, repayment takes place by means of expansionary borrowing, a monetary stimulus is provided. The government need not commit itself about the precise date of repayment and could choose this date according to the requirements of cyclical development.

Such argument is not, however, entirely convincing. If in

some stage of postwar development it is desirable and possible to embark on expansionary monetary policies, governments and central banks are free to do so regardless of whether legal commitments force them to adopt these policies. The legal commitment to settle the bill for interest or principal is necessarily a factor reducing the freedom of action. Only accidentally could the settlement of the bill be undertaken in the framework of policies which, with regard to both timing and magnitude of the settlement, corresponds closely to the requirements of a reasonable cycle policy. Present commitments may easily force the government to adopt policies in the future which will be distinctly harmful. In no event are commitments necessary to the selection of the appropriate policies. Therefore, the argument in favor of compulsory loan schemes is unconvincing so far as it runs in terms of the postwar adjustment. A good case can be made, on the grounds of social welfare, for the application to the low-income brackets, of a compulsory lending program instead of taxation; and, to the extent to which this program keeps marginal tax rates below certain limits, a good case can be made for it on the basis of efficiency; it may thus be justified in spite of possible postwar consequences. Moreover, if the amounts involved in the program are not excessive and if the date or period of repayment is flexible, there is a fair chance of avoiding substantial repercussions in the settlement of the bill. But there is not much logic in the argument that the appropriate handling of postwar problems requires present commitments of any kind.

The previous sections of the present chapter led to the conclusion that an ideal policy of war finance might require raising by individual income taxation a fund corresponding to about 40 billions in terms of the prices, the income level, and the war effort of the fiscal year 1943. Considering the circumstances discussed in the present section, the conclusion may be qualified as follows. Social considerations and efficiency might justify combining taxation with a compulsory lending scheme.

By adopting a compulsory loan scheme, the long-run burden of the low-income brackets may be diminished and at the same time marginal tax rates of almost confiscatory height may be avoided. It is desirable, however, to lend some flexibility to the date of repayment and to keep the amounts in the loan scheme within reasonable limits. The meaning of "reasonable limits" is not clear-cut, of course. Yet, it should be pointed out that raising a relatively small part of the war fund by this method already leads to a serious postwar problem. If, after the war, within some period extending over several years, repayments must be made at an average annual rate of, say, 10 billions, serious difficulties may arise. Redemptions of such a size can fail to have harmful effects only in intervals which otherwise would be characterized by strongly deflationary tendencies.

In the subsequent pages I shall not distinguish between income taxation proper and compulsory lending. The two will now be subsumed under "income taxes" in the broader sense. Compulsory lending may always be viewed as income taxation amended by postwar credits.

Individual income taxes.—If the present (May, 1942) price level were stabilized, the 40 billions which would have to be raised by individual income taxation would presumably turn out to represent between 30 and 35 per cent of the aggregate income payments of the fiscal year 1943. This would be true if aggregate income payments should rise in a similar proportion to that which has been assumed earlier for national income at market prices.[5]

---

[5] The difference between national income at market prices and national income at factor costs was discussed in chapter iii. Aggregate income payments fall short of national income at factor costs by net corporate savings—or exceed it by net corporate dissavings. In other words, to the sum total of income payments we have to add net corporate savings in order to arrive at the sum total of factor earnings (i.e., at national income at factor costs). To this latter magnitude we have to add the taxes paid by or through business firms if we would arrive at the value of net output at market prices, which is here conceived in such a manner as not to imply that firms use up, in producing their final output, the government services which "they buy with tax payments."

What tax rates would be capable of yielding a revenue corresponding to 30 to 35 per cent of income payments? On this question only two general statements can be made with any definiteness.

First, the rates required for such a yield would have to be of an entirely different order of magnitude from those contained in the Treasury proposals of March, 1942. The proposed rates are apparently expected to yield a revenue of approximately 8 billions. In addition to the proposals already submitted to Congress, an increase in Social Security payroll taxes is planned which is expected to yield another 2 billions. Whether this latter item should be considered as "taxation" proper or forced lending on the part of the insured is a matter of interpretation which we need not decide here since, for the purposes of the present analysis, these two methods of war finance are subsumed under a common heading. On the basis of present plans the yield of income taxation, in this broader sense, falls short of 10 per cent of income payments. To say that consequently a tax scale yielding 30 to 35 per cent of income payments would have to be about "four times as severe" is misleading, however; such a statement fails to reveal the full extent of the additional tax burden for the greater part of the population. If we want to tax income rather than wealth, it is impossible to increase a taxpayer's burden fourfold unless he now is taxed at a rate lower than 25 per cent. Increasing total tax revenue fourfold, beyond the level of the Treasury proposals of March, 1942, means, of course, raising the tax burden of the high-income brackets much less, and that of the lower brackets much more, than fourfold. At the same time it is misleading, although "correct" in the formal sense, to say that a person's tax burden becomes 20 per cent higher if the rate applied to him increases from, say, 75 per cent to 90 per cent. This is misleading because the more significant aspect of this rise should be characterized by the statement that 60 per cent of his income after taxes has been taxed away additionally. Raising a fund corresponding

Noninflationary War Finance 101

to 30 to 35 per cent of national income instead of less than 10 per cent requires an exceedingly severe rate of taxation; and the difference cannot be adequately described with mere reference to the 1:4 ratio.

Second, raising 30 to 35 per cent of income payments by income taxation requires a reduction of exemptions substantially below present levels. Estimates made by Hart, Allen, and their collaborators indicate that in 1941 less than 20 per cent of total income entered into the tax base.[6] About one-half of income was earned by recipients who are entirely exempt and substantially more than one-half of the remainder failed to enter into the tax base of the taxpayer on account of family exemptions, deductions of various character, and understatement. On the whole, exemptions (at present amounting to $750 for single individuals, and to $1,500 for married couples and $400 for each dependent) account for much the greater part of the difference between total income and the tax base. The same estimates would indicate that the lowering of exemptions as passed recently by the House of Representatives (to $500 for single individuals, and to $1,200 for married couples and $400 for each dependent) would still leave appreciably less than 30 per cent of aggregate income payments in the tax base. Obviously it is impossible to raise a fund corresponding to 30 per cent of national income by subjecting to income taxation a portion falling short of 30 per cent. The objective of noninflationary financing would make a very significant lowering of exemptions imperative.

These statements do not answer the question of the effective tax rates which would have to be applied to the various income brackets in order to make the income tax structure yield 30 to 35 per cent of income payments. The question cannot be answered with any high degree of precision, since the distribution of income in the now exempt brackets is not adequately

[6] *Paying for Defense,* chap. xv. The 90-billion income level is approximately that of 1941.

known. Changes in the distribution of income within the groups subject to taxation give rise to further difficulties.

In spite of this it may not be useless to indicate the type of tax structure which, on the basis of distribution estimates published by the National Resources Committee, could be expected to yield roughly 30 per cent of the national income. Calculations like these can, at best, provide some information about rough orders of magnitude. Considering that recent Treasury estimates of the yield of certain tax scales are not much at variance with the rough estimates derivable by the method to be sketched, we may reasonably hope that the method does provide some such information. Quite recently (in June, 1942) the Office of Price Administration concluded an estimate of income distribution for the years 1941 and 1942. Using these estimates would have led to very similar results.

The National Resources Committee, in conjunction with four other agencies, undertook an estimate of income distribution for the twelve months between the summer of 1935 and the summer of 1936.[7] They also published estimates of the share of income that would go to each bracket at levels of total income higher than that of 1935–36.[8] The estimates rest on alternative assumptions regarding the changes in the distribution pattern occurring as total income rises. It was estimated that if (a) total consumer income should reach a level of 80 billions, and (b) the proportionate distribution between the various sections of the population should remain unchanged,[9]

---

[7] *Consumer Incomes in the United States,* National Resources Committee, 1938.

[8] *Consumer Expenditures in the United States,* 1939, secs. 3–5.

[9] The proportionate distribution may, of course, have changed. The assumption of unchanged proportionate distribution is, however, not so bad as it would seem to be, at first sight, on the basis of the argument of chapter iii. It was argued there that the typical inequalities of both depressions and booms might fail to show up in their extreme forms during the war period. This points to a potential change in the distribution pattern. Yet the argument of chapter iii relates, so far as boom inequalities are concerned, to income after taxes, while the text, above, relates to income before taxes. Besides, this type of inequality was not characteristic of 1935–36. As to depression inequalities caused by un-

each income class would earn that percentage of total income which appears in column 2 of table 4 (see p. 104). The income classes should be interpreted as consisting of consumer units earning an income which lies between the limits indicated in column 1. A consumer unit is defined as a composite consisting of families and of single individuals, so weighted as to correspond to the numerical proportion in which persons live as family members and single individuals respectively.

If exemptions were reduced to $1,000 for families with two dependents, and if, aside from the family exemptions, all "consumer income" were taxable, then the tax rates appearing in column 3 of the table would yield a revenue corresponding to 34 per cent of aggregate consumer income. These tax rates would have to be applied, however, to the entire income of a consumer unit of average size, and not merely to the portion in excess of the exemption.

Presumably if the implications of the table are not entirely unrealistic, the rates appearing in column 3 would, under present circumstances, yield somewhat less than the 34 per cent of aggregate income payments shown here. Income in the fiscal year 1943 might flow at a rate roughly 50 per cent higher than that which would correspond to the annual figure of 80 billions. Call the 80-billion level "100 units"; then income in fiscal 1943 may be at a level of about "150 units." With income at 100 units, the tax scale of table 5 would have yielded 34 units. How many units might the same scale yield at an income

---

employment, it should be pointed out that these must have been substantially reduced by 1935–36, as against the trough of the depression to which the argument of chapter iii relates. This is true not merely on account of the increase in private output between 1932–33 and 1935–36, but also as a consequence of the W.P.A. and of relief. Moreover, the draft creates a group with relatively low incomes for the duration of the war.

In the National Resources Committee estimates here considered, constant population is assumed. This tends to introduce an upward bias into conclusions relating to average income and to tax yields because, on account of the population growth, the increased total income of the war period is divided between an increased number of persons rather than among an unchanging population. The appropriate correction is probably slight as compared with the margin of error in calculations like these.

level of 150 units? On the basis of such a tax scale about 60 per cent of the increase in income would go to the Treasury, if the proportionate distribution should remain unchanged. The weighted average of marginal rates (weighted according to the

TABLE 4
INCOME-TAX SCALE YIELDING 30 TO 35 PER CENT OF TOTAL INCOME PAYMENTS

1. Income class (dollars)	2. Percentage of total income earned by each income class	3. Tax rates (percentages)	4. Marginal tax rate when income rises from median of class to median of next higher class (percentages)	5. Percentage of total income yielded by taxation of each class (2 × 3)
Under 250	0.3	....	....	...
250–500	1.4	....	....	...
500–750	2.9	....	....	...
750–1000	4.7	....	....	...
1000–1250	6.1	10.0	34.8	0.6
1250–1500	6.8	14.5	40.1	1.0
1500–1750	7.0	18.5	44.8	1.3
1750–2000	6.6	22.0	46.0	1.5
2000–2500	11.4	26.0	50.8	3.0
2500–3000	9.8	30.5	53.8	3.0
3000–4000	11.8	35.5	58.0	4.2
4000–5000	6.2	40.5	64.3	2.5
5000–10,000	9.0	50.0	87.5	4.5
10,000–15,000	4.0	65.0	89.5	2.6
15,000–20,000	2.3	72.0	....	1.7
20,000 and over	9.7	85.0[a]	....	8.2
	100.0			34.1

[a] On the average, so that 85 per cent of the incomes belonging in this class is taxed away.

relative share of the bracket to which each marginal rate applies) lies near 60 per cent for a rise in income by one-half. Consequently, 30 units of the 50-unit increase would go to the Treasury. Should only this correction be undertaken, the yield would rise from 34 units to 64 units and this would correspond to about 43 per cent of the 150 units of income.

Yet it is necessary to undertake another correction, which is in the downward direction. A rather significant portion of total income fails to enter the tax base for reasons other than those accounted for in the preceding calculation. We took account of family exemptions. Aside from this, however, not all income payments reach invidulas. Moreover, the tax law allows certain deductions; and evasions cannot be excluded entirely. Hart, Allen, and their collaborators have estimated that on account of these factors about 16 per cent of total income remains outside the tax base.[10] This estimate relates to a 90-billion income level, but it may be assumed that the proportion is not very different for a 120-billion income level. Removal of about 24 units (16 per cent of 150 units) from the tax base would probably cut down the 65 units tax yield to 47 units. A large portion of the 24 units must be assumed to come from sections of the income structure where the marginal rate is high (more than the weighted average referred to above). If a marginal rate of about 70 per cent is associated with these 24 units, then their removal curtails the tax yield from 65 units to somewhat less than 47 units. This corresponds to 31 per cent of a total income of 150 units. By lowering deductions other than family exemptions the yield could be increased, of course. These estimates indicate, therefore, that a tax scale of the character here considered might actually yield a revenue corresponding to about 30 to 35 per cent of income payments.

As was said at the outset, calculations like these can, at best, provide information concerning rough orders of magnitude. We can state with certainty that the objective of raising an income tax revenue corresponding to 30 to 35 per cent of income requires a substantial lowering of exemption limits; also, this objective requires taxation at rates significantly different from those applied or proposed at present. No one could foretell with high precision what the required rates would be, although the experts of the Treasury could obviously come closest to making a good forecast.

---

[10] *Loc. cit.*, p. 147. Part of these items not entering the tax base are also excluded from the National Resources Committee's total "consumer income."

A final word on the degree of progressiveness reflecting itself in the scale discussed above: On the factual assumptions described in the foregoing pages the degree of progressiveness could be changed in one of two ways. Given the exemption limits, it would be possible to move upward faster in the lower brackets. In other words, the marginal rates could be higher in the low regions and then could be somewhat lower in the high regions without impairing the total yield. Aside from this, exemptions could be reduced even further, and, should this be done, marginal rates could be somewhat lower throughout. If exemptions were not allowed, even a linear tax of 30 to 35 per cent would be conceivable. As soon as an exemption limit exists it becomes logically imperative, however, to move upward rapidly because the tax rate cannot be high in the neighborhood of the exemption limit without making for a paradoxical marginal rate of more than 100 per cent. Consequently, for the total yield to become high, tax rates must necessarily be very high in the upper regions. As was pointed out, sharp progressiveness is not merely desirable but also necessary, once the lowest brackets are exempt. If lower progression is desired, it seems preferable to substitute a general sales tax for part of the income taxation considered above rather than try to accomplish such an objective within the framework of an income-tax scale yielding one-third of the total income. Does it seem justified, on these or other grounds, to reduce the share of income taxes in war finance and to rely partly on sales taxes?

Combining income taxes with a general sales tax may seem appropriate for one of three reasons. (1) It may be assumed that high individual marginal tax rates would reduce economic efficiency even if income taxation should be applied in conjunction with compulsory lending. In the next chapter it will be argued that this assumption probably is unjustified. (2) It may be assumed that a lower degree of progressiveness as such would increase the chances of agreement within the political community. This, too, seems unlikely. (3) It may be assumed that, once income taxation has reached a high degree, additional consumption taxes are more readily accepted than a further increase in income taxation, because consumption taxes do not draw directly on money income. This third assumption seems realistic, but since it relates to a specific type of irrationality it should be left out of account in the present chapter. A hypothetical government which, in carrying out the policies most nearly corresponding to the leanings of liberal public opinion, could afford to disregard the conditions of internal political equilibrium, would have no good reason to lower the degree of income taxation discussed in the foregoing pages and to apply sales taxes instead.

Deduction at the source.—In the present chapter we have discussed policies which might raise 70 billions, or slightly more, in approximately the following proportions:

40 billions by individual income taxation combined with some amount of compulsory lending;
13 to 14 billions by corporate income taxation and by borrowing from current corporate earnings;
6 to 7 billions by excise taxes;
5 billions by such borrowing as is offset by capital consumption in the civilian sector;
5 to 6 billions by expansionary borrowing.

The opinion was expressed that substituting sales taxation for some portion of the income taxes here considered could hardly be justified with reference to incentives, but that such a policy might have certain advantages—which will be discussed in the subsequent chapter.

It should now be added that the effectiveness of such a program would require the deduction of a large share of the individual income taxes at the source. Deduction at the source has advantages which distinctly outweigh its drawbacks in times like the present. The main advantage of prompt collection is that it prevents the formation of an inflationary revolving fund in the hands of the taxpayer. If taxes are collected with a substantial lag, the Treasury must bridge the temporary gap by borrowing, no doubt partly in the form of security sales to the banks. At the same time, the taxpayer has a fund at his disposal which, in spite of being "offset" by an increase in his tax liability, may circulate permanently in the economy. Assume that the tax on the 1942 income of an individual is x dollars higher than was the tax on the income he earned in 1941. If he pays his 1942 taxes in 1943, he may be viewed as paying these taxes out of 1943 income, just as he may be viewed as paying the 1941 taxes out of 1942 income. It follows that the x dollars, by which the tax on his 1942 income is in excess of previous tax liabilities, in a sense always remain in his possession. It is as though the Treasury were to lend him this amount and not withdraw the credit—assuming that he continues to earn income at a roughly unchanging rate.

Deduction at the source should, however, be limited to amounts approximately corresponding to the increase in tax revenue from one year to another. If the measure is applied to the entire tax revenue of a year, double taxpaying is involved to the extent of the tax on the preceding year's income. This would often lead to taxpaying out of sources other than current income. Moreover, collecting more than the year's tax out of the year's income would not even be a desirable objective. If the tax structure is adequate to forestall inflation, double taxpaying will have some deflationary consequences. If the tax structure is too low to prevent inflationary developments, the imposition of double taxpaying is a clumsy way of narrowing the gap. The method would presumably not be very effective, because the abnormal burden of the year of transition would be met out of sources other than current income to a relatively large extent.

The logic of the objections which must be raised against the present system of collection necessarily relates to the increase of taxes from one year to another, rather than to the entire tax revenue. In connection with a tax flow of constant size the whole problem would be meaningless. It would obviously be impracticable to achieve prompt collection of the tax increment of each individual income recipient. Yet, prompt collection cannot be applied to all categories of income anyway, and the entire tax liability of those subject to prompt collection need not be withheld at the source. For the economy as a whole, deduction at the source might well be limited to a figure roughly corresponding to the increase in the tax burden.

The difficulties standing in the way of prompt collection are administrative ones. It should be possible to overcome these obstacles wherever the income recipient is distinct from the source. The difficulties arise because residuals of tax liabilities must be settled after the close of the year in which the income was earned. As a consequence of the progressiveness of taxes and of various allowances, the current deductions frequently would not add up precisely to the final tax liability. In spite of the necessity of settling balances in the subsequent calendar year, it is conceivable, however, that deduction at the source would reduce the costs of collection for the Treasury. A substantial part of these costs would fall to enterprises rather than to the government. In a hypothetical economy without frictions, prices would rise unless the enterprises should be reimbursed for the entire cost by the Treasury. As things work out in reality, the shifting of these costs could presumably be prevented.

The potentiality of declining average productivity.—If, in order to carry out the economic war program, it should be necessary to utilize resources in such a way that real output per unit of physical factor input would decline, some increase in the price level would be called for, unless money earnings per unit of factor input were to decline. In this event it might "rationally" be justified to create new money at a slightly higher rate and to tax at a slightly lower rate than was envisaged in the preceding sections. To lower the money earnings of the factors of production is no requirement of rational policy, especially not in the armament industries. It is preferable to define inflation so as to have it mean in increase in the earnings per unit of factor input rather than an increase in the price level, because the stimulus to the diversion of resources into the wrong channels as well as the cumulative tendency are produced by a rise in prices only if money earnings rise at the same time. These two criteria coincide only if average productivity remains unchanged. If the average productivity of the single factors, conceived as consisting of units identically priced at present, declines, the avoidance of both "inflation" and "deflation," in the foregoing sense, presupposes higher prices. The qualification to which the preceding numerical analysis may become subject as a consequence of this consideration is presumably insignificant, if not negligible.

CHAPTER VI

Present Policies—Future Potentialities

● *The nature of the difficulties.*—The chief reasons why tax policies of the character discussed above are not actually adopted are genuinely political. The distribution of advantages or burdens in a complicated social system does not typically follow a clear-cut and easily understandable pattern. If the sum of the net advantages available to groups A and B is given, the granting of an "advantage" to group B is the same thing as the burdening of group A in favor of group B. Politically, however, there might be a great deal of difference between the direct and the roundabout way. The granting of net advantages to some distinct social group at the expense of other groups very frequently arises from privileges which apparently have been granted to all groups. Group A obtains tariff protection at the expense of group B, and group B receives a government subsidy which ultimately is at the expense of group A; or group A cannot be prevented from acquiring monopoly power, but, on the other hand, group B is granted cheap credit, and so on. To the rational observer it is the difference which matters; politics is not rational in this respect. These hidden balances are an especially significant factor in the internal equilibrium of totalitarian communities, but they play an important role even in the social process of democratic nations.

The imposition of almost the entire war burden in the form of income taxes would involve almost complete avoidance of the roundabout way. In no major war has this ever been attempted, and it is extremely unlikely that any of the governments waging war at present would try it. Economists should advocate heavy reliance on the direct method; and although each conceivable specific program will include controversial proposals, economists should have somewhere in their minds the notion of an "ideal solution" characterized by the use of income taxes except so far as equity or economic efficiency clearly justify other methods. Yet a sober point of view in social matters always implies some kind of balance between a belief in the freedom of social will and the notion that certain characteristics of the social world are "given." Consistent attempts to convince the public of the merits of an ideal solution may, at best, bring the actual methods somewhat closer to the ideal.

A government attempting to raise almost the entire war fund by direct taxation would presumably run into poltical difficulties that would be insurmountable, unless there should be a radical shift in public psychology. This is true not merely of the American government; it is just as true of allied governments and of enemy governments. An income-tax bill is a matter that easily provokes conflict over the distribution of the war burden. Social unity is not promoted by such a conflict. Representatives of each section of the income structure have "good arguments" by which it can be shown that the bill would overburden the brackets under consideration in comparison with other brackets. Everybody feels that he has been treated unfairly. The great advantages of other methods so far as politics is concerned are that they do not draw on the money income of the public and that the distribution pattern they tend to establish is very imperfectly foreseen. Rationally viewed, these are disadvantages. It is much preferable to tax away money income than to have it depreciate; and it is much preferable to distribute the war burden in a clear-cut and equitable manner than to take measures that will lead to some unplanned and largely unpredictable incidence. Yet one form of the so-called money illusion is precisely that the resistance to taxing away money incomes is substantially greater than the resistance to roundabout methods of burdening; and as to the incidence, an unpredictable distribution pattern is frequently preferred to a definite pattern which is felt to be disadvan-

Policies and Potentialities 113

tageous by a number of groups. An income-tax scale of the character discussed in the previous chapter would seem exceedingly onerous to almost all groups.

Circumstances inherently political are the chief cause of what may be called the roundaboutness of war finance. Now, it could be argued that a very high and progressive income tax scale, even if combined with compulsory lending, would reduce economic efficiency in a direct way, that is, not merely by way of its effects on social and political balance. I do not believe that a serious adverse effect would be felt; but the contention requires some consideration. Raising enough income-tax revenue would require high marginal rates in the middle and upper brackets unless exemptions should be dropped completely. That the height of marginal rates has an important bearing on efficiency cannot be denied. Our previous argument has taken account of this in two ways. It was suggested that corporate income-tax rates be kept at a level which would leave some of the profit stimulus to increased efficiency. High personal income-tax rates, and conceivably the limitation of dividend payments, would in any event make a large share of the corporate earnings available for war finance. Second, it was suggested that a compulsory lending scheme be used partly for the purpose of reducing the marginal individual tax rate in those regions in which the marginal rate would otherwise closely approximate 100 per cent.

It was argued above that these two proposals would prevent effects adverse to efficiency. Yet this argument, also, should be examined.

Combination of compulsory lending with taxation proper could not, for various reasons, fully restore the income stimulus to increased individual effort. It is not a matter of indifference whether a person whose earnings rise is left with more money after paying his taxes, or with the same amount of money plus a certain amount of nonnegotiable government securities. This is, in fact, an important consideration to which we have not thus far paid attention. Moreover, two further circumstances tend to limit the stimulus which could be provided by combining compulsory loans with a tax scale of the kind discussed above. The amount of compulsory lending, it has been emphasized, must not be allowed to become excessive if postwar complications are to be avoided. The limits within which a reasonable war-finance policy should remain cannot be determined with anything like precision; but if not much more than about 5 billions per year were to be borrowed in this fashion, and if the compulsory loan program were also to be used in order to alleviate the long-run burden of the lowest among the taxed groups, it would hardly be possible to set the ceiling to the marginal rate at a level lower than about 80 per cent. The scale discussed in the preceding chapter could presumably be so amended as to have tax payments replaced by loans, if the tax payment should correspond to a marginal rate of more than about 80 per cent. Calculations more refined than these might indicate a somewhat higher or lower figure. Yet obviously there are limits to the possibility of leaving a stimulus even in the form of nonnegotiable securities, unless postwar problems are entirely disregarded. At the same time, definite commitments on dates of repayment must not be made if the entirely unreasonable risk of having to repay in an inflationary period is to be avoided. Hence the income stimulus to increased efficiency, which could be provided by combining compulsory loans with severe tax scales, is necessarily limited. Marginal tax rates could be kept at some distance below 100 per cent even in the higher regions of the income structure, but in the higher regions the stimulus would be provided mainly in the form of nonnegotiable securities with no fixed redemption date.

In spite of these considerations, economic efficiency would not be likely to suffer from severe individual taxation extending over the war period. Marginal rates lying within the danger zone would be confined to the high-income brackets, including at the extreme the top section of the so-called middle brackets.

A scale like that discussed in the preceding chapter would not, for example, imply marginal rates of more than 80 per cent before an income level of almost $10,000 should be reached. So far as these high incomes are earned for personal services, they are usually earned by persons who may be looked upon as specialists. The general standing of these persons in their respective professions rises with their incomes. Officials get higher incomes when they are promoted; lawyers' and doctors' incomes rise when their services become more highly valued. An official would be irrational if he should fail to do his best to win promotion merely because, for the duration of the war, the addition to his income might be taxed away. His income after the war will presumably be higher for an indefinite period if he is promoted now. Even if after the war he were to leave his present position and accept another, the chances are that the quality of the alternative position would be better, the higher the rank he reaches in the course of the war. For this category of income recipients the long-run marginal tax rate remains at a reasonable distance below 100 per cent, even though the short-run marginal rate approximates its theoretical ceiling. A person whose income is partly determined by his history is better off in the long run if he is promoted than if he is not, even though marginal tax rates may be quasi-confiscatory for a number of years. Marginal rates of 90 per cent or even 100 per cent, if confined to the war period, tax away but a small share of the increased capital value of his earning power.

The thesis can be extended, with some qualifications, to the independent professions. If a lawyer or a doctor wants to have a profitable practice after the war, he takes serious chances by letting his competitors make use of present opportunities. It is easier to maintain a practice than to build it up. The argument may, however, be somewhat weaker for professions like these than for salaried officials, because the failure to produce a full effort is more certain to have long-run consequences for the one group than for the other.

Hence, it does not seem likely that severe and progressive individual taxation combined with a compulsory lending scheme would eliminate the economic incentive to increased efficiency. In the higher brackets the short-run financial incentive would no doubt be weakened significantly even though some of this stimulus could be retained throughout the income structure. The long-run incentive would, however, remain important in the income classes in which the short-run stimulus would become small. These factors, in conjunction with the strength of the patriotic motive, would tend to maintain the quantity and quality of the individual effort even should some solution of the kind discussed above be adopted.

The problem of corporate effort has different characteristics. If marginal corporate tax rates should approximate 100 per cent, there would frequently be a conflict between the long-run interests of enterprises and wartime efficiency. The main emphasis should probably not be placed on the possibility that the war emergency might end before armament plants should be written down and hence that actual loss might attach to war investments if additional reserves could not be accumulated out of profits. This difficulty can be met—apparently it *is* met—by such methods of financing and by the granting of such amortization quotas as render it possible to write down war plant and war equipment out of tax-free reserves within a reasonable time. Yet, under quasi-confiscatory marginal tax rates for corporations other difficulties become inescapable. Present outlays yielding very little additional income in the long run would become profitable because increased current outlays, if accountable as costs, would not substantially affect the size of profits after taxes. This would imply a direct premium on certain types of waste, and such a policy would directly stimulate rather than reduce additional money spending on the part of corporations.

Frequently, moreover, the postwar position of an enterprise, as against that of an individual, would not be improved by an

Policies and Potentialities 117

increased wartime effort. This long-run substitute for the short-run profit motive would not be universally present. An automobile factory now producing tanks will not be the stronger on the postwar automobile market the more efficiently it produces tanks at present. The analogy between corporate effort and personal effort is incomplete in this respect. Furthermore, so far as quasi-confiscatory marginal taxation leads to a conflict between wartime efficiency and private interest, a conscientious person will more readily forget about his own comfort than about the interests of others whom he is supposed to represent. Besides, he cannot be held responsible for having sacrificed his own personal comfort whereas he may in the long run have to bear the consequences of having ineffectively represented an enterprise. It is frequently said that providing incentives to owners is less important than providing incentives to managers. Yet management is under a very strong pressure once the interests of the nation and those of the enterprise coincide. Few managers can afford to be considered unpatriotic persons and poor managers at the same time.

The question may also be raised whether it would not be preferable to drop the distinction between excess and normal profits and to raise the same revenue by taxing profits indiscriminately at progressive rates. On considerations of equity, acceptable arguments can be made for and against excess-profits taxes. On balance, I believe, somewhat more can be said for than against the discrimination involved in the taxation of excess profits as such. The case for this type of taxation may be said to rest on the notion that a firm has a weaker claim to retain high profits which are likely to have been earned in consequence of a war than to retain high profits which it has also been earning in normal times. The case against this discrimination would have to rest, so far as equity is concerned, on the notion that it is as justifiable to earn high profits by supplying an improved wartime market, as it is to earn *the same profits* by supplying a wartime market which did not happen to improve. It appears to me that the argument is somewhat stronger for than against the taxation of excess profits as such, but less conclusive, even on grounds of equity alone, than is frequently believed. So far as the incentive to efficiency is concerned, the indiscriminate, progressive taxation of profits is preferable to the taxation of excess profits, because the latter concentrates on the margin. If the same revenue obtained by corporate income taxes proper plus excess-profits taxes were derived from the indiscriminate taxation of profits, the same share of total profits could be taxed away without pushing marginal tax rates as high as they actually are pushed under a discriminatory system. The rates on excess profits essentially are rates applied to the margin and consequently they bear directly on incentives. If the top rates on excess profits are kept reasonably below 100 per cent, then it is possible to take into account the balance of the arguments previously mentioned which would seem to favor some discrimination against the "excess," and at the same time to retain the incentive to higher efficiency. If, however, rates on excess profits are pushed to the immediate neighborhood of 100 per cent, the incentive is abandoned for the sake of a case which, even in terms of equity alone, is not *very* strong. It may be added that the weakness of the argument does not favor attempts to apply the excess principle to the taxation of individuals, where the difficulties in ascertaining the difference between war and prewar incomes would be very great or insuperable.

Unfortunately, the economic limitations of reasonable corporate taxation tend at the same time to reduce the "politically feasible" degree of individual taxation. Even if marginal tax rates for corporations should be raised to a level of 100 per cent, the comparison of the position of individuals with that of "business" would still provide a political argument against the severe taxation of individuals. It is possible to rule out the profit incentive to higher effort by a 100-per cent marginal rate, and it is possible to tax normal profits at high rates, but this does not mean that, in the politically and sociologically relevant sense, one has ruled out "high profits." It would still be necessary to allow for rapid amortization of war investments, and it still would be impossible to combine an efficient war-production program with an extensive purge of accepted accounting methods and of accounting departments. The profit incentive to more efficient performance would be ruled out, but corporations still would be "making much money."

The limits of individual income taxation are mainly political. If the political community could be persuaded to accept a tax scale of the kind considered above, the individuals of whom the nation consists would presumably continue to produce services without loss of efficiency. Even those who disagree in this respect would have to admit that their objections, based on the potential harmful effects of high marginal individual tax rates, could be met by combining income taxes with sales taxation. The limits of the taxation of business profits, on the other hand, are "economic" to a higher degree. Confiscatory marginal rates in the field of corporate taxation presumably would lead to a loss of economic efficiency. Nevertheless a 100-per cent excess-profits tax is more likely to be closely approximated than a truly radical individual income-tax scale; for the excess profits tax imposes a direct burden on a narrow group only, which here happens to be in a weak bargaining position. The tax in all probability is indirectly harmful to the war economy as a whole.

The sharpness of the distinction between political and economic obstacles should not, however, be overestimated. An attempt to break a strong resistance which is essentially political may be unwise in times of acute emergency, and economic efficiency may be reduced indirectly as a consequence of the disruption of political and social equilibrium. It is apparently impossible to induce political communities to reach an agreement on the direct distribution of the entire burden of a major war. The attempt to press such an agreement beyond certain limits may be less expedient than the attempts to deal with the residual in some other way. Yet it must not be forgotten that the problem is one of proportions. The residual, if it grows beyond certain limits, cannot fail to produce grave consequences.

Actual policies of war finance.—The budget message of the President, submitted to the joint session of Congress on January 7, 1942, and the more detailed proposals which Secretary Morgenthau submitted to the Ways and Means Committee of the House of Representatives on March 3, imply a combination of different war-finance policies. The main difference between this combination of policies and that discussed in the preceding chapter appears in the Administration's proposal to raise by means of personal income taxation a fund corresponding to only about 8 billions, that is, to about 7 per cent of the national income expected for the fiscal year ending with June, 1943. It has been announced that further proposals will be submitted which will raise an additional 2 billions in the form of increased Social Security contributions. This additional amount could be viewed as compulsory lending on the part of the insured. Since the income payments of the fiscal year 1943 are expected to reach a level of about 120 billions, personal income taxation including this type of compulsory lending would yield a fund falling short of 10 per cent of income payments. According to the same proposals, corporate income taxes, including the excess-profits tax, might yield another 10 billions, and if to the yield of these taxes we add that of excises, gift and estate taxes, and miscellaneous minor items, a total internal revenue of about 26 to 27 billions results. The Treasury will apparently require more than 70 billions. If taxes are not raised beyond the level now contemplated, somewhat more than 60 per cent of the total fund required will have to be raised by the means of borrowing operations. The main difference between this program and the policy discussed above consists in the degree of expansionary borrowing, which, in

Policies and Potentialities

the Treasury proposals, takes the place of two-thirds of the income taxation (and compulsory lending) considered in the preceding chapter.

It is unlikely that the Treasury proposals will be accepted without modification. The changes Congress is likely to make will be indicated later. The original proposals, however, remain of interest not merely because most of the changes will probably be relatively small, but also because the proposals reflect the initial wartime policy of the Treasury.

The Treasury would leave a family with two dependents tax exempt up to an annual income of $2,300. Taking average deductions (in addition to family credits), the limit of tax exemption would probably be reached around $2,500. On the basis of any reasonable extrapolation from prewar estimates, it must be assumed that this income is well in excess of the "most probable income" earned by an American consumer unit (i.e., well in excess of the mode of the frequency distribution). An income of $2,500 for a family with two dependents will presumably turn out to be slightly less than the average (arithmetic mean) income earned by American consumer units in the fiscal year 1943. But families of average size earning the average income would, at most, have to meet a tax burden of negligible magnitude. According to the Treasury proposals, families with two dependents would be taxed at an effective rate of about 3 per cent on an income of $3,000. Taxation would essentially be confined to above-average incomes.

A large section of the income groups from which the tax revenue of about 8 billions is to be collected would be taxed at a moderate rate only. Families of average size would have to meet a tax burden of 8 per cent on an income of $4,000 and the effective rate would rise to about 11 per cent for incomes of $5,000, to about 20 per cent for incomes of $10,000, to 33 per cent for incomes of $20,000, and to 68 per cent for incomes of $100,000. The marginal rates implied in Secretary Morgenthau's proposals would reach a level of 30 per cent in the range between $6,000 and $8,000, a level of 50 per cent around $20,000, and of 80 per cent around $70,000. Considering that a fund corresponding to about 60 per cent of national income will be required for war finance, these tax rates are lenient throughout. Not only is taxation confined to above-average incomes, but the rise in the rate of taxation, as reflected by marginal rates, is also rather slow up to about $20,000.[1]

The rates of corporate taxation originally proposed by the Treasury come close to those consistent with the policy discussed in the preceding chapter.[2] The proposed rate and scope of excise taxation is smaller, however. A sharper increase in the taxation of liquor and tobacco would seem to be appropriate. Furthermore, while the proposed system of excises contains some items which might curtail the demand for scarce services, these items are not very important. The entire excise structure, not including customs, might be assumed to yield about 4 billions, unless inflationary developments raise the yield.

Since the expenditures of the federal government during the fiscal year 1943 are expected to exceed 70 billions, the total internal revenue of 26 to 27 billions would provide somewhat less than 40 per cent of the funds required, and the rest would have to be met by borrowing. There can be no doubt that a large part of this borrowing would tend to have inflationary effects. The Administration in May, 1942, froze almost the entire price structure at its level of March, 1942, in an attempt to prevent its borrowing operations from actually producing the inflationary effects. Labor services and those agricultural products the prices of which at the farm have not yet reached 110 per cent of parity are the most significant exceptions to the

---

[1] The House of Representatives proposes to lower exemptions, as indicated on p. 101. The scale, as modified by the House, would still place a very slight tax on the average income. Moreover, the rates of the House are somewhat more lenient than those of the original Treasury proposals in the middle and upper brackets. On the whole, the modifications of the House would reduce total internal revenue even below the level contemplated by the Treasury. The difference exceeds 2 billions.

[2] Concerning the Treasury proposals see p. 93.

Policies and Potentialities

general freezing order.[3] Even if combating inflation were merely a matter of issuing the appropriate price regulations, these two exceptions would reduce the chances of success, because it becomes difficult to deny approval to price increases once costs have been bid up on the markets for factors of production and for raw materials.[4] Moreover, it is questionable whether a legal ceiling on wage rates would of itself effectively prevent the further rises in labor costs. Allocating labor may become necessary not merely for the direct purpose of speeding up war production, but also because competing firms have

---

[3] More precisely: such prices as could not be stabilized at March levels without preventing farm prices from reaching the highest of the four levels defined in Section 3a of the Emergency Price Control Act. The other three levels are: (1) the average price of the listed commodity during the period July 1, 1919–June 30, 1929; (2) its price on October 1, 1941; and (3) the price on December 15, 1941. Yet 110 per cent of parity is the effective level for almost all prices. This essentially means 110 per cent of that *ratio* between the prices of farm commodities and the prices of all items entering into the budget of farmers which existed in the period 1909–1914.

[4] The General Maximum Price Regulation was promulgated on April 28, 1942, and, with respect to the greater part of the price structure it went into effect in May. In general, the ceiling price is the highest price charged by individual sellers to buyers of any given category in March, 1942. Aside from those pointed out in the text, the following exemptions should be mentioned: armament products purchased by the federal government; professional services in general; books, magazines, newspapers; entertainments, service in hotels, restaurants, bars; fresh fruits and vegetables. Before the General Maximum Price Regulation was adopted, more than 100 ceiling schedules were already in effect. These maximum schedules, just like the G.M.P.R., were issued on the basis of the Emergency Price Control Act, which became law in January, 1942. Making the "freeze" universal would require an amendment to the Act. Prior to the passing of the Emergency Price Control Act, the defense agencies attempted to keep certain prices from rising beyond ceiling levels defined *ad hoc*, but they had no legal power to enforce their decisions. Installment credit, however, has been subject to restrictive regulations by the Federal Reserve Board since September 1, 1941, on the basis of an executive order of the President issued in August. Moreover, the defense program was implemented by direct interference with the allocation of resources whenever this seemed necessary. Priorities, direct allocation, limitation of the production of certain commodities, prohibition of the use of certain raw materials in specific industries, and complete prohibition of the production of certain commodities were, and are, the main measures under this heading. These measures relate to the allocation of material rather than of human resources. The allocation of labor has not thus far been subjected to government regulation. This increases the danger of labor costs being bid up by competing entrepreneurs, especially under "cost-plus" contracts with the government which guarantee to the entrepreneur a price covering actual costs plus a profit margin.

a strong incentive to bid up labor costs. Labor allocation would render it necessary to fix wages, not merely to place a ceiling on them, in order to prevent firms from reducing the wages of the labor force allocated to them.

It seems plausible to assume that in the absence of direct consumers' controls at least 25 billions of the 45 billions to be borrowed would constitute a net addition to the money stock. The present stock of money is somewhat in excess of 50 billions. Considering that at the same time the supply of consumers' goods will be declining, the planned fiscal policies may bring forth a primary tendency toward inflation at a very high annual rate. This tendency will have to be suppressed by direct controls, that is, mainly by rationing of consumers' goods and the control of their prices.

The noninflationary fraction of the 45 billions to be borrowed is that which is offset by current gross saving. Total gross savings consist of savings out of net income plus depreciation and liquidation funds. That part of the gross savings not required for replacement and for private net war investment tends to offset the inflationary effect of Treasury borrowing.

In the absence of rationing and price control, savings out of net individual income would not be high. In normal times a high percentage of the income accruing at the level of full employment would be saved, but the real income in advanced stages of the war period will be low in terms of consumers' goods. Even the real consumption of nondurable items will have to be reduced substantially. If merely this were taken into account, the aggregate individual net savings might become negative. The public might dissave in an attempt to maintain its consumption standards. But if we take the virtual unavailability of certain new durable consumers' goods for granted, a slight positive figure might result. When the question is raised concerning what individual savings would amount to in the absence of rationing and of price control, we still may take the conversion of plants and the complete unavailability of certain durable commodities for granted.[5] Some portion of the money which cannot be spent on these goods tends to be saved genuinely because many of the nondurable commodities are exceedingly distant substitutes of the durables (no less distant substitutes than are savings). Nevertheless, it would be unreasonable to expect a significant amount of genuine savings out of individual incomes in a period in which real consumption must be substantially curtailed. We may even be too optimistic when guessing that in such circumstances the saving ratio out of individual incomes could reach 10 per cent, corresponding to about 12 billions.[6] A higher rate of saving could only be enforced by direct consumer controls, which would prevent the public from maintaining consumption standards through increased spending on scarce commodities.

To the individual savings should be added corporate savings out of net earnings. These amounted, in 1941, to 2.5 billions. The sharp rise in corporate taxation will presumably prevent net corporate savings from becoming significant. As a further item of gross savings we have, however, to add that part of the depreciation and liquidation funds which will be used neither for replacement nor for private war investment, and which was previously estimated to be about 5 billions. It follows that in the absence of direct consumers' controls gross savings might at best amount to about 20 billions. This means that of the 45

---

[5] By now (May, 1942), complete cessation of the production of the following durable goods has been ordered: refrigerators, radios, phonographs, sewing machines, vacuum cleaners, washing machines. New automobiles are, of course, unavailable to practically the entire population.

[6] In the absence of consumer controls the attempt to maintain consumption standards would result in a rise in prices, and inflation would get under way. Inflation is like a distinctly regressive tax, and consequently savings would be reduced somewhat less sharply than, *ceteris paribus*, under progressive taxation. It might be pointed out that according to estimates published by Gilbert and Bangs in the May, 1942, issue of the *Survey of Current Business*, individual savings seem to have amounted only to about 5 per cent of total income payments at the trough of the depression; and that the ratio seems to have been less than 10 per cent in 1939, when consumption was higher than it will be in advanced stages of the war. The estimate of the text would in all probability be too high, were it not that part of the income normally spent on certain durable consumer goods now genuinely tends to remain unspent.

billions to be borrowed no less than about 25 billions would tend to come out of inflationary sources.

The actual policy, as officially announced, is one of heavy reliance on direct consumers' controls. This policy will apparently be characterized by an effort to transform the 25 billion, or more, of inflationary borrowing into noninflationary borrowing by the means of a general price ceiling and of rationing, implemented by a restrictive regulation of consumer credit.[7] The rationing will apparently be undertaken by the dealers themselves wherever the excess of demand over supply at the ceiling price will not exceed a certain margin. Where higher excess demand occurs, the government will issue ration cards.

Theoretically, an all-inclusive and completely effective system of rationing and price control could preclude any inflationary gap. If all commodities and services were so rationed and their prices so fixed as to force the public, by the process of elimination, to save 25 billions in excess of what it would tend to save voluntarily, then the inflationary gap would obviously be closed by these additional savings.

In reality, no system of consumers' controls is all-inclusive, and no system is completely effective. It seems convenient to distinguish three degrees of effectiveness.

Effectiveness of the first order exists to the extent to which the controls induce the public to save and either buy government securities or repay bank loans.[8] If the controls were 100

---

[7] The regulation relating to consumer credit is known as Regulation W of the Federal Reserve Board. Minimum down payments (usually 33⅓ per cent of the price) and maximum maturities (usually 12 months) are prescribed for installment loans. The regulation has been extended (in May, 1942) to charge accounts with respect to a comprehensive list of articles and prescribes that payment may not be deferred beyond the tenth day of the second calendar month after the month of the sale. The maximum maturity of single-payment loans not exceeding $1,500 is fixed at 90 days, aside from certain exceptions. See *Federal Reserve Bulletin*, May, 1942.

[8] In this connection reference should be made to the suggestion of Professor M. R. Benedict. In the framework of a compulsory loan program he would reduce the obligation of the individual to lend to the government by the amount which is used for private debt retirement. See "The Control of Postwar Deflation," *Bank of America Business Review*, May, 1942.

Policies and Potentialities 127

per cent effective in this most pretentious sense of the term, the government could avoid an increase in the money supply, except for a relatively small initial amount which would serve as a revolving fund. This fund would, however, be saved with a slight "Robertsonian" lag, and it would continuously flow back either to the government against newly issued securities or to the banks in repayment of loans. A constant rate of deficit spending would not, in these circumstances, require any creation of new money, because the revolving fund would either be continuously buying the newly issued securities or continuously serving to decrease bank loans by the amount of the government borrowing from banks. An increasing rate of deficit spending would require the creation of new money only because the revolving fund would have to be increased. The size of the revolving fund necessary to finance any given volume of deficit would depend on the length of time it would take for the new money to flow back either into the market for government securities or to the banks in repayment of loans. Complete effectiveness of the first order would not merely imply that lending to the government and the repayment of bank loans prevent consumption demand from increasing; whenever the physical supply of consumers' goods should decline, lending to the government and the repayment of bank loans would, in conjunction with the insufficient taxation, have to curtail consumption demand correspondingly.

Effectiveness of the second order may be said to exist to the extent to which the controls induce the public to save and to accumulate idle deposits. Complete effectiveness in this sense would also prevent the new money from becoming demand for consumers' goods and, further, would lead to a curtailment of consumption demand whenever the supply should shrink. But the public would retain its savings in the form of cash hoards and the effectiveness of the controls would not reduce the government's borrowing operations from banks. This type of effectiveness is distinctly less desirable than is effectiveness of the first order, because the supply of money is more easily controlled than its velocity. Once velocity has reached very low levels, a tendency to dishoard may be extremely difficult to counteract. The controls may become ineffective later in the war, or a postwar inflation may become inevitable.

Effectiveness of the third order may be characterized by the ability of the controls to direct spending from controlled to uncontrolled commodities and services. Complete effectiveness of this order would not induce any saving, but it would prevent additional spending on controlled goods and would curtail expenditures on these commodities whenever their supply should decline. Considering that on the supply side practically all commodities and services stand in at least a distant relationship of competition with war materials, effectiveness of merely the third order—unassociated with effectiveness of the first and second order—might involve grave dangers. The reader's attention may be directed, in this connection, to the "Kalecki plan," which, by rationing individual consumer expenditures, would implicity ration as a group those commodities not rationed specifically.

The controls in this scheme may be called *ineffective* to the extent to which they fail to keep the demand for controlled goods at a level determined by their supply and by their ceiling prices. To this extent they have no effectiveness in any of the three senses defined above. Ineffectiveness can reflect itself either in the existence of "black markets," or in the necessity to adjust official prices upward in order to prevent "black markets" from acquiring significance. It can also reflect itself in such upward revisions of ceiling prices as may become inevitable on account of political considerations, including those which lead to exempting basic cost items from the controls. Ineffectiveness in another sense, not bearing directly on the over-all situation, also exists to the extent to which certain consumers are capable of acquiring more than their rations and others are forced to go with less.

Policies and Potentialities

In this connection the question arises whether the deterioration of the quality of products at unchanging prices should be considered a phenomenon essentially inflationary, reflecting the ineffectiveness of controls. It may be suggested that the answer depends on whether the physical output of the inferior product per unit of physical factor input is higher than that of the original product. If the output per unit of input is higher, then the phenomenon is essentially inflationary because money income per unit of factor input increases. Under these circumstances, a smaller fraction of the flow of factor services is capable of yielding the same total money income as that which was yielded previously by a larger fraction, since it takes a smaller input to produce x units of the inferior product than to produce x units of the original product. Consequently, a stimulus is provided to the diversion of resources in the particular channels here under discussion and the increased profits earned in the industries producing the inferior products will tend to render the process cumulative in the Wicksellian sense. If, however, the output per unit of factor input is the same for the inferior product as previously for the original commodity, then the failure to reduce the price will not increase the money income per unit of factor input. In this event, the process has only one characteristic in common with inflation: the consumption burden is distributed over the community in the proportion in which individuals are buyers of the commodity. Now, a phenomenon which has only this characteristic in common with inflation resembles a consumption tax more than an inflationary process; for consumption taxes are in a like relation to inflation. The additional characteristics of inflation—such as the stimulus to the diversion of resources in certain channels, and the cumulative tendency—appear, with respect to quality deterioration, only if prices are maintained in spite of the fact that one unit of factor input produces a greater quantity of the inferior than of the superior commodity; and only then should the deterioration of quality at unchanging prices (reflecting the ineffectiveness of controls) be considered an "inflationary phenomenon."[9]

It should be added that ineffectiveness of consumers' controls clearly tends to reduce the effectiveness of priorities and of allocations and thereby tends to reduce the efficiency of the war economy. The profitability of violating priorities and allocations increases as the effectiveness of consumers' controls decreases. Moreover, not all types of effectiveness avoid these dangers completely, especially not in the longer run. Effectiveness of merely the third order does not reliably prevent the leaking out of war resources into certain uncontrolled sections of the "civilian" economy. Effectiveness of the second order involves the danger that the hoards become activated in some later stage. Effectiveness of the first order avoids these difficulties, but, as compared with taxation, it too has the disadvantage of creating a transfer problem for the postwar period.

Priorities and the allocation of resources tend, in themselves, to exclude the possibility of ineffectiveness with respect to specific commodities only if they result in the almost complete elimination of certain consumers' goods from the market and if the remaining supply is put on the market by a small number of sellers. The consumers' controls relating to new automobiles can, for example, hardly prove ineffective, in the foregoing sense, to any substantial extent. A small turnover by a relatively small number of firms can be controlled with a high degree of effectiveness. In the discussion of the tendency to save we have assumed the effectiveness of controls like these. We have even implied that in the absence of consumers' controls commodities like these would be taken entirely off the commercial market and that consequently the savings resulting from the inability to buy certain durable consumers' goods may be included in the amount the public genuinely tends to save in the given circumstances regardless of the effectiveness of consumers' controls.

---

[9] Cf. the definition of inflation in fn. 1, p. 2, and on p. 110.

Policies and Potentialities

The question of *how* effective the American direct consumers' controls will be in these various senses of the term is not one which could even tentatively be answered *a priori*. Complete effectiveness of the first order can obviously not be expected. Some effectiveness of the first order and a substantial degree of effectiveness of the second order seems quite likely. The effectiveness will, no doubt, be partly of the third order only. We must also be prepared for some amount of ineffectiveness. Generally speaking, it may be expected that direct consumers' controls become the less effective the higher the monetary pressure against which they have to operate. This monetary pressure results from that part of the deficit which does not genuinely tend to be offset by gross savings; in other words, the monetary pressure may be measured by that amount of additional saving which the consumer controls would have to "induce" in order to rule out the inflationary effects of the deficit. If the monetary pressure is small, the controls may have almost complete effectiveness of the first order. As the pressure increases, effectiveness of the second and third orders partly takes the place of effectiveness of the first order, and some degree of ineffectiveness ceases to be avoidable. The size of the monetary pressure which the controls have to overcome is not the only variable on which their effectiveness depends, but obviously it is significant. It could hardly be contested that the American controls will have to operate against a very high monetary pressure unless taxation is raised substantially beyond the level now planned.

A fair appraisal of the policies outlined in official announcements since Pearl Harbor requires the addition of two more comments: first, it should be noted that there are signs that the Administration plans to press for higher taxation in the future;[10] and second, that the existence of an inflationary gap

---

[10] Both the President's radio address of April 28, 1942, and the statement of considerations published by the Office of Price Administration in connection with the General Maximum Price Regulation emphasized the importance of diminishing the excess spending power of the public.

of similar relative size is a common characteristic of numerous war economies.

For example, Great Britain in the fiscal year ending in March, 1942, raised slightly over 40 per cent of her total government expenditures by means of taxation.[11] Somewhat more than 50 per cent of the British internal revenue was raised by income taxation, including the excess-profits tax. According to the American Treasury proposals for the fiscal year 1943, the share of expenditures to be raised by taxation would be almost the same; the share of individual plus corporate income-tax revenue in total internal revenue would, however, be distinctly higher (about 70 per cent), because profits other than excess profits are not subject to double taxation in Great Britain.[12] They are not taxed as profits *and* as individual dividend incomes as in the United States and many other countries. The standard income tax is deducted at the source—that is, it is paid by the companies—and need not be paid again by the shareholder on his dividends. The 1941–42 British income-tax revenue, excluding that from the excess-profits tax, corresponds to more than 40 per cent of the yield of all taxation. The American individual income-tax revenue as planned for fiscal 1943 will probably be about 30 per cent or 40 per cent, according as the planned increase in Social Security contributions is disregarded or included. It seems justifiable to include in the American revenue those items which represent compulsory lending, since part of the British income-tax revenue will also be refunded after the war.[13]

In interpreting these figures it should not be overlooked that government expenditures correspond to a higher propor-

---

[11] The following pages rely heavily on recent estimates published in *The Economist* and based, to a large extent, on the British White Paper on war finance. See the issues of *The Economist* for January 3 and April 11, 1942.

[12] Excess profits are taxed at a rate of 100 per cent, but 20 per cent will be refunded after the war, on certain conditions, and will be subject to income tax once more.

[13] British postwar credits extend to such individual income-tax payments as would not have been due had the prewar family exemptions and earned income credit been retained, and, furthermore, to 20 per cent of the excess-profits tax.

Policies and Potentialities

tion of national income in Great Britain than they will in this country for fiscal 1943. In the fiscal year ending with March, 1942 the expenditures of the central government (4.7 billion pounds) corresponded to no less than 75 per cent of the 1941 national income at factor costs (6.3 billion pounds);[14] in the United States they apparently will correspond to about 60 per cent. Consequently, total tax revenue, corresponding to similar proportions of fiscal expenditures, amounts to a higher proportion of national income in Great Britain than is now planned for this country—more than 30 per cent as against less than 25 per cent. Income-tax revenue, including the revenue from profits taxes, might amount to about the same proportion of American national income in fiscal 1943 as the corresponding British proportion in the fiscal year ending in March, 1942 (16 to 18 per cent). Since in Britain profits other than excess profits are taxed but once, however, it is more meaningful to compare the American individual income-tax revenue with the British revenue from income taxes excluding the yield of the excess-profits tax. This comparison would indicate that the British income-tax yield is much higher in proportion to national income at factor costs, that is, in relation to aggregate factor earnings, than the American yield is expected to become on the basis of the Treasury proposals (14 per cent as against 7 to 8 per cent). The British figures will presumably not change to any significant extent in the present fiscal year, although the share of income taxes in total revenue might decline slightly since a planned 10-per cent rise in total spending will be financed in a relatively high proportion by increased excises.[15]

---

[14] Figures relating to national income at factor costs are used here, because in the subsequent comparison of individual income-tax yields it is preferable to relate British and American yields to factor earnings rather than to output at market prices. It would perhaps be even preferable to take aggregate income payments, but the difference between income payments and national income at factor costs is negligible for the present purpose (see footnote, p. 99). British income at market prices is estimated at 7.3 billion pounds for 1941.

[15] On the other hand, Congress may modify the Treasury proposals in such a manner that the yield of individual income taxes will become slightly lower.

A comparison such as the foregoing tends to suggest that the British consumers' controls have to overcome an even greater inflation potential than that to which the American controls will be exposed, since government expenditures correspond to a higher share of national income in Britain than is planned for the United States, while the tax revenue does not correspond to a higher share of total expenditure.

The conclusion would be incorrect, however. It seems quite likely that the British controls operate against a smaller monetary pressure than that which would arise in this country if the tax revenue for fiscal 1943 should not be increased beyond 26 to 27 billions and a deficit of about 45 billions should result. A fairly large portion of the British war expenditures is associated with capital consumption from abroad. Lend-lease shipments are not included in the figures relating to British expenditures, but the adverse balance of payments and the spending of British assets in the United States contributed close to 900 million pounds to the value of goods allocated to the war and consumed in Great Britain. To this extent the deficit is not of much immediate inflationary danger, since at worst a very small fraction of the sterling balances paid out for foreign assets tends to be spent on consumption. So far as central banks or overseas governments acquire sterling balances (or gold) there is no such tendency, and even so far as British residents acquire sterling for foreign assets no tendency to consume is generated which would be comparable in magnitude with the tendency to consume income. Besides, keeping track of these funds is also easier than control of the use of incomes. This, of course, is not the only constituent of British spending which fails to create "income" in the hands of the direct recipient of the pounds. Expenditures on existing domestic assets also do not give rise to income in any direct sense. But capital consumption from abroad is the most significant British item of this kind and this item has no counterpart in American war finance. If these 900 million pounds are sub-

Policies and Potentialities

tracted from the British deficit of fiscal 1941–42, then the resulting 1.9 billion pounds is found to be smaller in relation to several significant economic magnitudes—such as income, the stock of money, internal revenue—than are the corresponding ratios for the United States. Nevertheless, it is true of the British as well as the American policy that substantial inflationary tendencies originating from the deficit financing of the war are intended to be checked by direct consumers' controls.

How successful is the British rationing and price-control system in enforcing a substantially higher rate of gross saving than that which would naturally tend to prevail? That effectiveness of the first order is incomplete appears clearly from the circumstance that the stock of money has risen significantly. The money stock seems to have risen by roughly 40 per cent since the outbreak of the war and a considerable portion of this rise has occurred rather recently. Since early in 1941, effectiveness of the first *plus the second* order has, however, suppressed the greater part of the inflation tendency. In other words, the controls do not induce the public to buy bonds and to repay bank loans at a rate which would render it possible to avoid a rise in the stock of money. During the fiscal year ending with March, 1942, the money stock was increasing at an appreciable rate although the rate of government spending had not increased substantially since the last quarter of the preceding fiscal year; but a substantial portion of the new money was hoarded. This "effectiveness of the second order" reflects itself in the circumstance that the rate of consumption spending has not risen since the last quarter of 1940. It must, however, be pointed out that effectiveness of the first *plus* the second order has not suppressed the *entire* inflation tendency even since January, 1941, in which period the controls have been much more effective than previously; for the time rate of consumption spending has remained approximately unchanged since late in 1940 while the physical supply of consumers' goods has declined. The decline of the physical supply was mainly a consequence of the fact that additional government spending on domestic products and services, implying the withdrawal of British resources from the civilian sector, was substituted for part of the government spending on foreign capital consumption. (Foreign capital consumption declined after passage of the Lend-Lease Act.) Had effectiveness of the first plus the second order been complete, the rate of consumption would have had to decline by roughly 10 per cent since late in 1940. This decline would have corresponded to roughly 400 million pounds per annum. The circumstance that this decline has not occurred reflects itself but slightly in a rise of the official price indexes. For the rest, it may reflect itself either in effectiveness of the third order, that is, in additional spending on uncontrolled goods, or in some degree of ineffectiveness, that is, in illegal spending on controlled goods. It probably reflects itself in both to some extent. Since the beginning of 1941 both the cost of living index and the wholesale price index have remained fairly stable. Since the outbreak of the war the cost of living has risen between 25 and 30 per cent and the wholesale price index slightly over 60 per cent, but most of this rise (26 and 50 per cent, respectively) had occurred by the end of 1940.

On the whole, it would seem that the policy of controlled inflation is being carried out in Britain with as much success as could reasonably be expected. This apparently is the feeling of the majority of competent observers, although they do not overlook the weaknesses. The degree of emphasis placed on these weaknesses varies. "There are one or two signs that 'potential' inflation exists, e.g. runs on unrationed goods, black markets in certain commodities, and some speculation in land," writes Mr. Brinley Thomas;[16] "The national economy is escaping from the strait-jacket in which the Chancellor [of the Exchequer] believed he had tied it," writes *The Economist*.[17]

---

[16] Brinley Thomas, "How Britain Is Avoiding Inflation," in *Financing the War* (Tax Institute, Philadelphia, 1942), pp. 269-283, esp. p. 282.

[17] Issue of January 3, 1942, p. 4.

Policies and Potentialities

Reliance on inflationary methods on the one hand and on an elaborate system of controls on the other is a characteristic of British and American war finance and of the war finance of the democracies in general. But it is essential to realize that the obstacles standing in the way of avoiding, rather than controlling, inflation are equally substantial in the totalitarian countries. Germany spends on the war at a current rate corresponding to more than half her national income, and, in addition, acquires by force those constituents of her war effort which are analogous to the foreign-capital consumption and Lend-Lease aid of Britain. And Germany, too, borrows rather than raises by taxation more than half her government expenditures. In the fiscal year 1940–41 taxation seems to have yielded only about 40 per cent of total government spending, and it seems that this ratio will remain roughly the same for the current German fiscal year. The rest was raised through borrowing, to a large extent directly or indirectly from banks. Moreover, her tax structure is less progressive than those of the leading democracies. Income and property taxes, taken as a whole, seem to contribute, however, a similar proportion to German internal revenue as to American or British. The official price indexes have been practically stable since the outbreak of the war, but quality has deteriorated substantially and violations appear to be fairly frequent.

How far the concepts used in this discussion are meaningful when applied to the Russian economy is not clear. In 1937, Russian defense expenditures already corresponded to roughly 20 per cent of the national income figure, according to official estimates. By 1940 this proportion rose to 45 per cent. A rate of defense spending corresponding to 50 per cent of net output was apparently reached, if not surpassed, by the time Germany attacked the Soviet Union.

Weaknesses of controlled inflation: future potentialities.— The following are perhaps the most conspicuous disadvantages of the method of controlled inflation.

1) Effectiveness of the controls is apt to be incomplete. Obviously no complete effectiveness of the first order can be expected. Effectiveness of the second order, resulting in a substantial rise of the idle money stock, implies the danger of ineffectiveness in the later course of the war and also the danger of postwar inflation. Effectiveness of the third order implies some of the dangers, and ineffectiveness all the dangers, of uncontrolled inflation. These dangers are twofold. It becomes exceedingly difficult to prevent the leaking out of war resources into the civilian sector, and the distribution of the war burden becomes highly inequitable.

2) Even assuming a hypothetical system of controls, with 100 per cent effectiveness of the first order, inflationary war finance would lead to a substantial increase in the public debt and create a transfer problem for the postwar period. This is a disadvantage of the method as compared with taxation.

3) The extensive policing activities necessary to enforce the controls effectively are apt to become unpopular in a country with democratic traditions. If, however, policing activities are kept within narrow limits, the effectiveness of the measures is apt to be low.

4) The effort required to enforce the regulations is costly not merely in terms of money but also in terms of human resources.

All these drawbacks are serious. As to the third disadvantage mentioned, it may be objected that wars cannot be won without sacrificing temporarily some of the civil liberties which democratic communities are accustomed to enjoy. This is quite true; but it does not follow that procedures of a totalitarian flavor should be chosen where other procedures could be relied upon. As was argued in the preceding chapters, it is inherently impossible to assure the efficiency of the war economy and to distribute the war burden in an equitable manner without introducing direct controls. These objectives require controls at all theoretically conceivable levels of taxation. But although

Policies and Potentialities

some amount of direct control is indispensable, it should be realized that the scope of the controls and the intensity of the policing effort required to enforce them depend very largely on the amount of money to be frozen by these methods. The effectiveness of the controls during the war also depends largely on the magnitude of the monetary pressure which has to be overcome; and the danger of postwar inflation, too, becomes the more acute the higher are the amounts which the public was forced to save for the duration of the war. All drawbacks of the policy of controlled inflation become increasingly pronounced as the inflation potential which has to be suppressed increases. The degree of inflation to be controlled in the United States by direct methods will become very substantial if tax rates are not raised beyond the levels contained in the Treasury proposals. It follows that it might be preferable to accept the disadvantages of certain other policies before relying on controlled inflation to the degree now contemplated.

First of all, it should sooner or later become politically possible to increase individual income taxes substantially beyond the rates contained in the Treasury proposals. Earlier in this discussion the view was stated that the effective limits of individual income taxation are mainly political. This means that it would probably be possible to adopt for the duration of the war an extremely severe personal tax scale without loss of efficiency, especially if taxation should be combined with compulsory lending. Nevertheless, tax scales such as the one discussed in chapter v are not adopted—for political reasons. A fight for a tax scale of this kind would very likely be a hopeless one. But a fight for a substantial further increase of individual income tax rates cannot *a priori* be considered hopeless.

The fear of inflation will presumably rise and thereby will prepare the ground for more energetic fiscal policies. The burden will be more generally felt, and the public will come nearer to realizing that the war cost is measured rather by the relative size of war expenditures on current output than by the size of tax bills. It should then become easier to demonstrate that increased income taxation distributes the war burden more equitably and avoids the inefficiency created by inflation, but that it does not increase the total burden of the war. In this connection it is worth while to recall that the rates of the British income-tax structure exceed the planned American rates by a significant margin, and that British income taxes are withheld at the source. If the present exchange rate of 4 : 1 is taken, the comparison results in the following figures. The exemption limit is less than half as high in Britain as in the United States, both for single persons and for married couples (in Britain, $320 and $560, respectively; here, $750 and $1,500, respectively).[18] Married couples with two dependents are taxed at about five times the proposed American rate around an income level of $3,000; at about three times the planned American rate around $5,000; at about twice the rate at $10,000; at slightly over 1½ times the rate around $20,000; at 1.2 times the planned American rate around $100,000. These differences would remain significant even if the comparison were based on a rate somewhat more favorable for the pound than is 4:1. Consistent propaganda for higher income taxation might sooner or later yield beneficial results.

Although a lowering of exemption limits and an increase in individual income-tax rates should prove attainable in the future course of the war, the inflationary gap will remain substantial if additional consumption taxes are not introduced at the same time. We do not know where the political limits of income taxation lie, but it seems certain that they lie well below the level at which the inflationary gap would be reduced to insignificance. The gap would remain significant even if the British rates were introduced. It seems likely, however, that the politically feasible limits of individual income taxation lie distinctly below the level attained in Britain. The

---

[18] Exemptions will apparently be increased slightly in Britain for the fiscal year 1942–1943.

Policies and Potentialities 141

British adopted this income-tax structure at a time of most immediate danger, when the enemy was only twenty miles from their homeland and still seemed invincible. We may believe that an analogous situation will not arise for the United States, and this probably implies that the resistance against direct methods of burdening will remain higher.

At this point the problem arises: Is the distribution of the burden more equitable if regressive taxes, such as a general sales tax, are relied upon to narrow the gap, or is it more equitable to omit this type of taxation and to rely to a correspondingly larger extent on the method of direct rationing alone? And how is the efficiency of the war economy affected by the choice between these alternatives?

The answer depends on what estimate is made of the effectiveness of direct controls and on appraisal of the postwar difficulties to which the temporary freezing of excess money may lead. If it were possible to disregard the disturbances to which excessive reliance on direct controls may lead during and after the war, the answer would be obvious. Rationing would then be a more equalitarian method, since it reduces the consumption of the wealthy by an appreciably higher margin than that of the poor. Distribution under an all-inclusive system of rationing and price control would differ from the theoretical limit of equal distribution only in that not everybody could afford to buy his entire ration of all goods. Wealth in addition to that required for the purchase of all rations would be of no use for the duration of such a system. By combining rationing with a progressive income tax the equalitarian effect of the policy is not diminished, unless the income tax cuts into such incomes of the lower brackets as could be spent for rations in a manner compatible with the physical requirements of the war program. Since it is obvious, however, that the war program requires curtailment of consumption by the low-income brackets as well as the high, a substantial lowering of tax exemptions would not diminish the equalitarian effect of rationing. The rations will in any event have to be so fixed as to reduce consumption by the low-income groups.

One might object that there is a difference between taxing away income from the low brackets or leaving them with temporarily frozen money which they may use after the war. The objection is correct, but it could be taken care of by applying a compulsory loan scheme, rather than taxation in the narrower sense, to those brackets which are normally exempt. This is what the British have done. But while, as a measure consonant with a liberal policy, the combination of rationing with income taxation (plus compulsory lending) is clearly desirable, reliance on regressive taxes raises a different problem. Here there is a real conflict. The regressive tax, such as a general sales tax, may also be said to tax away from the lower income groups money which these groups should not be allowed to spend on consumers' goods. But, assuming an equitable system of rationing, the higher income groups have more such "excess" money than the lower, and the regressive tax takes away more excess money from the lower groups than from the higher. Furthermore, it also curtails the real consumption of the very lowest income groups, whose standard of living might remain unaffected so far as the physical requirements of the war program are concerned. In other words, it is inconsistent to say that the equalitarian objectives pursued by a rationing program would be impaired by a substantial increase in income taxation, but it is not necessarily inconsistent to argue that these objectives might be impaired by heavy reliance on consumption taxes.

The reason why we believe that a certain amount of regressive taxation should nevertheless be accepted can be expressed as follows. Once the political limits of direct taxation (plus compulsory lending) are reached, the choice is one between "controlled inflation" and indirect taxation of a regressive kind. The political limits of direct taxation will probably be reached at a level too low to reduce the dangers of "controlled

Policies and Potentialities 143

inflation" sufficiently. The dangers of controlled inflation are largely the same in kind, though not in degree, as those of inflation pure and simple. To the extent to which the controls are ineffective during the war, genuinely inflationary phenomena are generated; and the temporary character of the controls is likely to result in a genuinely inflationary effect after the war. Thus, *there seems to be a range within which the evils of regressive taxation may be substituted for the evils of inflation.*

The usual types of regressive taxation are both less regressive and less harmful, so far as efficiency is concerned, than inflation. Sales taxation, for example, need not apply, strictly speaking, to all commodities, or, if the tax is general, the rate need not be the same for all types of goods.[19] It is possible to discriminate, within limits, in favor of the poorest groups of the population. Inflation does not discriminate; once it is under way, the distribution of burdens gets out of control. The burden is imposed by an automatic and cumulative rise in the cost of living with which disposable money incomes fail to keep pace. Both wartime and postwar inflation come to an end in some state of the postwar process, but this again cannot take place without causing a heavy shock to the economy and large-scale unemployment, also borne mostly by the poor. Sales taxes and excises can be cut down gradually after the war as resources are shifted back to the civilian sector. Regressive taxes are antisocial as compared with income taxes, but they are much less antisocial than inflation. It is preferable to implement direct controls by taxing away excess money from all groups of the population, including the low-income groups, through income taxation rather than through sales or excise taxation. But it is much preferable to tax away some of the excess money by means of sales taxes and excises rather than leave the amount of the excess at an unmanageable level.

---

[19] The British Purchases Tax applies a rate of 16⅔ per cent, on the wholesale level, to items other than luxuries, and twice (in the future, probably three times) this rate to luxuries. Necessities in the stricter sense are entirely exempted.

It should be emphasized that inflation is more undesirable than the usual types of regressive taxation not merely where the distribution of burdens is concerned. Inflation creates speculative opportunities which compete with the requirements of the war program and thereby may seriously affect the efficiency of the war economy. If it becomes distinctly more profitable for producers to allocate their resources to the production of civilian commodities the prices of which "run away" than to the production of war materials the prices of which are kept down, it is difficult to prevent the leaking out of factors of production from the war sector into the civilian sector. Not merely the direct consumer controls, but also the entire system of priorities and allocations, has then to operate against a rising monetary pressure. Consumption taxes, while raising ultimate prices, do not increase the earnings obtainable through the production of consumers' goods.

The conclusion is that individual income taxes should be pushed to their outside political limit, and furthermore, that consumption taxes should be accepted as a welcome substitute for inflation. The reason why consumption taxes will presumably be attainable at a stage in which a further increase in income taxation could not be accomplished has more to do with the indirectness than with the regressiveness of the taxes under consideration. The political weight of the groups who are favored by progression and are hurt by regressiveness is substantial in this country. These groups would be capable of blocking regressive taxation just as other groups are capable of preventing progressive taxes from being pushed beyond certain limits. The main political advantage of consumption taxes lies in their indirectness rather than in their regressiveness. The psychological burden is smaller if prices rise than if money is taxed away so long as the rise in prices is not sharp enough to induce the public to change its appraisal of the value of money. The appraisal of the "value" of money is obviously rigid ("sticky") within rather wide limits. Now, as these pages are written, the cost of living is already 15 per cent in excess of its 1939 level, but few people have yet revised their attitude toward the dollar. A person who is offered a $1,000 job does not typically feel that he is offered about 15 per cent less than one thousand units of the prewar currency. Yet, even if the cost of living had remained unchanged, he would certainly feel that $850 was much less than $1,000.

To say that a person is "equally well satisfied" with $1,000 regardless of whether the cost of living is 15 per cent higher or lower would be an overstatement. But it is true, within a rather wide range, that most of the loss imposed by rising prices fails to reflect itself in a feeling of impoverishment. The dollar symbolizes and measures wealth, and its value in terms of commodities must change substantially before the public begins to draw a clear distinction between, say, 1942 dollars and 1943 dollars. Consumption taxes are accepted in circumstances in which additional direct taxes could not be introduced because they capitalize on this stickiness of the psychological measure of wealth in terms of money, or, as we may say alternatively, on the flexibility of the psychological measure of wealth in terms of commodities. Inflation also starts with capitalizing on this phenomenon, but its cumulative character soon produces a situation in which a substantial revision of the money measure does take place. From 1915 to 1920, for example, the cost of living almost doubled. A little more than half the total rise occurred before and during the period of hostilities; the rest reflected the phenomenon of postwar inflation. Changes like these obviously do lead to a distinction between different dollar measures of wealth. It is suggested, therefore, that the emphasis should not be placed exclusively on the inferiority of consumption taxes to the taxation of income. Part of the emphasis should be placed on the superiority of consumption taxes to inflation.

Finally, the suggestion may be repeated that highly scarce commodities be taxed on used as well as on new markets. The case for preventing relative price movements is weaker than is generally realized. The price system misbehaves when its general level displays violent movements, but it merely performs its normal function when the prices of highly scarce commodities increase in relation to more abundant commodities.

We would not, however, go to the point of concluding that the demand for highly scarce commodities should be limited solely by allowing their relative prices to rise to the equilibrium level. Usually, a combination of excises leading to some rise in the relative price, with direct controls stabilizing that higher price, would seem the appropriate policy. In an abnormal period of limited duration, such as a war period, the usual habits of the population continue to provide the measure of normalcy from which the departures are measured. Consequently, we have here a conflict between two notions of normalcy, especially for commodities which are usually consumed by the low-income groups as well as by the high. On the one hand it is "normal" for relative price movements to direct consumption into the fields of relative abundance. On the other hand, it remains true of certain highly scarce commodities of a war economy that they are "normally" abundant and, therefore, relatively inexpensive. This would justify reliance on relative price movements to some limited extent and on direct rationing plus price control for the rest. Exclusive reliance on relative price movements in the limitation of the demand for commodities of high scarcity seems warranted only when the commodities are luxuries the consumption of which, even in normal times, is confined to the high-income groups. Complete exclusion of relative price movements would seem to be justified only for necessities in the stricter sense. The notion of necessities in the stricter sense is not clear-cut, but few scarcities of the American war economy would fall in this category.

Partial reliance on relative price movements would greatly facilitate the task of the price-control authorities. If high excises were imposed upon commodities of more than average

Policies and Potentialities 147

scarcity, the higher price (including tax) would be easier to enforce. The attempt to keep all prices at an unchanging level is unlikely to be successful. If, in the absence of specific taxation, prices of certain commodities rise on new or on used markets, then windfall profits are created which could have been taxed away more easily and more fully by consumption taxes than by the *ex post* taxation of profits. Moreover, while the addition of a tax to the prices under consideration does not stimulate the withdrawal of resources from the war sector of the economy, high profits on the production of scarce consumer goods do provide this unwelcome stimulus.

Generally speaking, the effectiveness of an anti-inflation program depends on the close coördination of direct controls with fiscal policies. Considering the marked trend toward government regulation which has been characteristic of recent decades, there is not much danger that the importance of direct controls will be underestimated. It is the economists' task to create and maintain awareness of the fact that direct controls are insufficient in themselves. They are complements of, not substitutes for, truly energetic fiscal policies. Outlawing inflation will not of itself produce good results. Only within certain limits, and only temporarily, is it possible to outrule by decree the consequences of inflationary war finance.

Postscript on Recent Developments

● *Taxation.*—As this study goes to press (in October, 1942) the tax bill submitted to Congress in March, 1942, is not yet enacted, but it is now possible to indicate the main changes undertaken by Congress in the course of a debate that extended over seven months. These changes do not, in any essential respect, call for a reconsideration of the argument presented in the preceding pages. Income-tax exemptions will amount to $500 for single individuals, to $1,200 for married couples and, in addition, to $350 for each dependent. The individual income-tax rates originally proposed by the Treasury have been slightly raised for the low-income groups and somewhat reduced for the high; at the same time the Victory levy has been added to previous taxes, while consideration of proposals relating to higher Social Security contributions has been rejected for the time being.

The Victory levy is to be paid by all income recipients earning more than $12 per week ($624 per year). The levy amounts to 5 per cent of the excess of income over this exemption. Single individuals receive a postwar credit to the extent of 25 per cent, and married couples to the extent of 40 per cent, of the levy falling on them (with 2-per cent additions for dependents). Five hundred dollars for single individuals and $1000 for married couples (with $100 additional for each dependent) is the upper limit of the postwar credit. For debt retirement, premium payments on life-insurance policies previously acquired, and for war-bond purchase the amounts corresponding to the postwar credit are made available immediately. The levy is to be withheld at the source. The total income-tax revenue, including the revenue from the Victory levy, may be expected to reach the yield contemplated in the original Treasury proposals. Table 5 indicates the combined tax burden.

The income and Victory tax levied on consumer units of average size earning the mean income (probably about $3,000) is likely to be distinctly below 10 per cent if all deductions are taken into account; and the "most probable income," which as a consequence of the skewness of the income distribution is smaller than the mean income, will be practically, although not literally, tax exempt.

TABLE 5
INCOME TAX AND VICTORY LEVY AS APPLICABLE TO A MARRIED PERSON WITH TWO DEPENDENTS AND MAXIMUM EARNED-INCOME CREDIT
(Dollars)

Income	Income tax	Victory levy	Total tax and levy
600	....	....	....
800	....	8	8
1,000	....	18	18
1,200	....	28	28
1,500	....	43	43
1,800	....	58	58
2,000	....	68	68
3,000	154	118	273
5,000	507	218	725
10,000	1,646	468	2,114
20,000	5,154	968	6,122
25,000	7,461	1,218	8,679
50,000	21,480	2,468	23,948
100,000	55,298	4,968	60,266
500,000	369,472	24,968	394,440
1,000,000	765,472	49,968	815,440
2,000,000	1,557,472	99,968	1,657,440

SOURCE: Data published in the *New York Times*, September 9, 1942.

It remains true that the British and also the Canadian rates are significantly higher throughout the income structure, even if the Victory levy, including the postwar credit, is added to the American income tax. It also remains true that British individual income taxation is roughly twice as high for incomes of about $10,000, and that this proportion declines in the higher range approximately as indicated on page 140, above;[1] but the British burden becomes a *high* multiple of the Ameri-

[1] For $100,000 incomes the proportion is about 1.4:1. This proportion takes into account the Victory levy, but not the additional income taxes levied by some

can only in the low-income classes. The Victory levy and the lowering of exemptions tends to keep the ratio in the neighborhood of 2:1 (instead of 3:1 and 5:1) for the middle incomes considered on page 140 above. The discrepancy between Canadian and United States rates is almost equally significant for an important range of incomes. In this connection it should be pointed out that Canada raises at present one-half of her expenditures by taxation, and that a further increase of this ratio is planned for the future.

The modification by Congress of the original Treasury proposals concerning corporate taxation are not those which would be consistent with the points of view developed in chapters v and vi of this study. The tax burden was concentrated more on the *margin* of earnings. The excess-profits tax was raised to 90 per cent, of which 10 per cent will conceivably become a postwar credit; and the upper limit of the tax (including the surtax) on normal profits was lowered from the 55 per cent included in the Treasury proposals to 40 per cent. Intramarginal earnings are treated more leniently, marginal earnings more severely, than was originally planned; the total revenue will be roughly the same.

Some of the Treasury proposals concerning increased excises were adopted, and others were rejected. Assuming that both the individual income taxes (including the Victory levy) and the corporate taxes will yield slightly over 10 billions and that the yield from excises will not drop below 3 to 4 billions, total revenue, including that from gift and estate taxes and from miscellaneous smaller items, will be between 25 and 30 billions. The Administration will probably advocate further taxation as soon as this shall seem politically practicable.

---

of the states. If these were included, a proportion of about 1.2:1 would result for $100,000 incomes in New York State. For middle incomes the state income taxes are very slight even in the states which do tax income. Aggregate state and local tax revenues now correspond to about 8 per cent of American income payments, whereas the corresponding figure for British local tax revenues is about 4 per cent.

Wage rates and agricultural prices.—The Act of October 2, 1942, empowered the President to stabilize wage rates at recent levels, agricultural prices at a level corresponding to parity rather than to 110 per cent of parity.[2] However, for those agricultural commodities the 1942 prices of which were above parity the 1942 prices are the lowest that may be stabilized. The Executive Order destined to accomplish these objectives was issued immediately. If ceiling orders are to prevent the upward spiraling of prices, parity is preferable to 110 per cent of parity, because it is lower. It should not be overlooked, however, that the ideal of parity prices was declared once more to be the basis of long-run agricultural price policy. Effective adoption of this principle would amount to freezing an important section of the *relative* price structure over a period of thirty years or more. Demand and costs in different industries change significantly in relation to one another. The policy of "parity prices" constitutes an attempt to exclude the relative price system from the process of adjustment.

The war-production program.—The Budget Director announced recently that the estimates concerning war expenditures in the fiscal year 1942 were revised upward by about 10 per cent. The chairman of the War Production Board reports, however, some lagging of actual production behind the program. It does not seem likely that the assumptions of chapters i and iv–vi of this study, which concern the war effort in relation to total output, should prove significantly too low. On the basis of an announcement of the chairman of the War Production Board in September, 1942, these assumptions should be considered realistic. According to some observers, they might even prove too high.[3] If in the first full fiscal year of American participation commodities and services corresponding to about 60 per cent of national income at factor costs are allocated to the war, we may be satisfied.

---

[2] Cf. fn. 3, p. 123.
[3] Cf. p. 58.

APPENDIX I: TABLES

TABLE 1
INDUSTRIAL PRODUCTION
(Adjusted for seasonal variation, 1935–1939 = 100.)

Commodity	1939 Aug.	1939 Nov.	1940 Feb.	1940 May	1940 Aug.	1940 Nov.	1941 Feb.	1941 May	1941 Aug.	1941 Nov.
Industrial production, total	105	124	116	116	124	134	144	154	160	166
Manufacturing, total	108	125	116	116	126	137	148	160	166	173
Iron and steel	113	163	124	126	163	171	179	184	185	191
Machinery	104	123	123	124	138	152	177	206	224	229
Aircraft	190	241	283	331	460	600	741	876	1113	1340
Automobile bodies, parts, and assembly	96	91	111	109	121	125	143	152	141	142
Railroad cars	74	122	158	121	127	166	182	218	236	264
Locomotives	102	98	101	102	123	162	204	256	306	338
Shipbuilding	133	142	150	164	213	226	307	384	485	645
Nonferrous metals	112	153	142	127	146	155	173	189	189	190
Lumber and products	105	121	114	112	114	127	135	132	140	135
Stone, clay, and glass products	113	120	113	113	119	130	158	141	154	161
Textiles and products	111	128	108	104	113	135	143	157	154	156
Leather and products	103	108	98	88	97	107	108	123	121	134
Manufactured food products	111	110	113	111	114	117	120	123	132	141
Alcoholic beverages	96	98	96	100	91	96	108	114	128	109
Tobacco products	110	110	106	110	106	113	116	119	118	132
Paper and products	112	134	114	127	124	125	128	142	147	153
Printing and publishing	105	117	108	115	110	110	114	122	129	136
Petroleum and coal products	110	120	116	114	113	118	122	125	130	135
Chemicals	100	111	111	114	115	117	124	136	145	149
Rubber products	112	126	119	122	115	132	153	162	130	134
Fuels	89	118	112	115	112	113	113	121	129	128
Metals	105	131	130	134	123	148	148	152	148	146

SOURCE: *Federal Reserve Bulletin.*

TABLE 2
NONAGRICULTURAL EMPLOYMENT
(Adjusted for seasonal variation. In thousands.)

Industry	1939		1940				1941			
	Aug.	Nov.	Feb.	May	Aug.	Nov.	Feb.	May	Aug.	Nov.
Nonagricultural employment, total.	34,678	35,538	35,288	35,139	35,747	37,364	38,314	38,824	40,100	40,604
Manufacturing..................	9,478	10,129	10,035	9,798	10,160	10,957	11,335	11,886	12,614	12,736
Mining........................	826	860	845	854	862	833	846	877	923	892
Construction...................	1,251	1,271	1,186	1,196	1,256	1,669	1,132	1,698	1,666	1,924
Transportation and public utilities..	2,955	3,012	2,999	3,006	3,058	3,053	3,087	3,192	3,302	3,310
Trade.........................	6,176	6,238	6,181	6,224	6,282	6,698	6,662	6,781	7,027	7,043
Financial service and miscellaneous.	4,124	4,157	4,164	4,157	4,175	4,125	4,158	4,188	4,246	4,266
Government....................	3,724	3,728	3,735	3,761	3,811	3,886	3,951	4,059	4,179	4,290

SOURCE: *Federal Reserve Bulletin.*

Appendix I

TABLE 3
Percentage Distribution of National Income by Industrial Divisions, 1939, 1940, 1941

Division	1939	1940	1941
Total national income	100.0	100.0	100.0
Agriculture	8.1	6.9	7.8
Mining	1.8	2.2	2.2
Manufacturing	23.2	26.0	29.2
Contract construction	3.0	3.2	3.9
Transportation	7.0	7.0	6.8
Power and gas	2.0	1.9	1.7
Communication	1.3	1.3	1.1
Trade	13.6	15.0	14.0
Finance	8.6	9.1	7.9
Government	14.1	13.2	12.4
Service	12.5	9.6	8.5
Miscellaneous	4.8	4.5	4.6

Sources: Milton Gilbert and Dwight B. Yntema, "National Income Exceeds 75 Billion Dollars in 1940," *Survey of Current Business*, June, 1941; *New York Times*, March 7, 1942.

TABLE 4
Percentage Share of Capital Formation in Aggregate Output Flow

Constituent	1929		1939	
	Percentage of net output	Percentage of gross output	Percentage of net output	Percentage of gross output
Gross capital formation[a]	24.4	21.7	22.1	20.3
Net capital formation[a]	12.1	10.8	8.9	8.2
Consumers' equipment[b]	11.0	9.8	9.9	9.1

[a] Not including consumers' stocks other than residential building. The other durable consumer goods are included under Consumers' Equipment. Source: T. N. E. C. Monograph No. 37—*Savings, Investment and National Income*.

[b] Source: George Terborgh, "Durable Goods Expenditures in 1940," *Federal Reserve Bulletin*, February, 1941.

TABLE 5
AVERAGE HOURS WORKED PER WEEK AND LABOR HOURS PERFORMED IN MANUFACTURING INDUSTRIES

Hours	1939		1940			1941		
	Aug.	Nov.	Feb.	May	Aug.	Nov.	Feb.	May	Aug.	Nov.
Average hours worked per week	38.0	38.5	37.3	37.2	38.4	38.6	40.0	40.8	41.0	40.3
Labor hours[a] (1939 = 100)	100.8	109.1	103.7	101.3	108.8	115.5	125.7	135.1	143.9	143.3

[a] Derived by multiplying employment in manufacturing by average weekly hours. An index of labor hours was formed from this product.

SOURCE: *Federal Reserve Bulletin.*

Appendix I

TABLE 6
PERCENTAGE INCREASES OVER THE PRECEDING MONTH IN WHOLESALE PRICES AND COST OF LIVING

Prices and costs	1941											1942		
	Mar.	Apr.	May	June	July	Aug.	Sept.	Oct.	Nov.	Dec.	Jan.	Feb.	Mar.
Wholesale prices, all commodities...	1.1	2.1	2.0	2.6	2.0	1.7	1.7	0.7	0.1	1.2	2.6	0.7	0.9
Manufactured products...	0.8	1.5	1.9	1.7	1.7	1.6	1.4	1.2	—0.1	0.9	1.9	0.6	0.8
Semimanufactures...	2.2	2.0	1.5	1.4	0.3	1.8	0.9	—0.4	—0.2	0.4	1.8	0.3	0.3
Raw materials...	1.8	2.9	2.8	4.9	3.0	1.7	2.7	—0.3	0.6	2.3	4.1	0.9	1.2
Farm products...	1.8	3.9	2.7	7.5	4.5	1.9	4.1	—1.1	0.7	4.5	6.4	0.5	1.5
Cost of living[a]...	0.4	1.0	0.7	1.7	0.7	0.9	1.8	1.1	0.8	0.3	1.4	0.8	1.2
Food...	0.5	2.2	1.5	3.7	0.8	1.2	2.5	0.8	1.3	0.0	2.7	0.5	1.5
Clothing...	1.7	0.3	0.4	0.5	1.5	2.0	3.6	1.6	1.1	0.9	0.8	2.6	3.7
House furnishing...	1.2	0.8	0.8	2.0	2.0	1.4	2.8	2.1	1.0	1.0	0.9	1.7	1.2
Rent...	0.0	0.3	0.3	0.1	0.3	0.2	0.5	0.7	0.3	0.4	0.2	0.2	0.3
Fuel, electricity, and ice...	0.1	0.3	0.1	0.3	0.9	0.9	0.5	0.3	0.0	0.1	0.1	0.0	0.1

[a] U. S. Department of Labor Index.
SOURCE: Survey of Current Business.

TABLE 7
PERCENTAGE INCREASE OVER THE PRECEDING MONTH IN INDUSTRIAL PRODUCTION
(Adjusted for seasonal variation. 1935–1939 = 100.)

Particulars of production	1941											1942		
	Mar.	Apr.	May	June	July	Aug.	Sept.	Oct.	Nov.	Dec.	Jan.	Feb.	Mar.
Industrial production, total	2.1	−2.0	6.9	3.2	0.6	0.0	0.6	1.2	1.8	0.6	2.4	0.6	0.0
Iron and steel	3.4	−1.6	1.1	0.5	0.5	0.0	3.8	−0.5	0.0	2.6	−2.6	1.0	2.6
Machinery	4.5	4.9	6.2	3.9	0.9	3.7	1.3	1.8	−0.9	5.2	2.9	2.8	3.9
Aircraft	3.6	6.5	7.1	6.2	7.2	11.6	8.2	7.1	3.9	†	†	†	†
Locomotives	5.9	9.7	8.0	9.4	9.6	−0.3	4.2	5.0	0.9	†	†	†	†
Railroad cars	−2.2	10.1	11.2	6.9	0.0	1.3	5.5	11.6	−5.0	†	†	†	†
Shipbuilding (private yards)	9.1	5.4	7.9	12.3	9.1	3.9	15.5	13.2	1.7	†	†	†	†
Automobile bodies, parts, and assembly	−0.7	−12.7	22.6	5.9	4.3	−16.1	−5.0	9.0	−2.7	−15.5	−1.7	−11.0	0.0
Lumber and products	−5.2	3.1	0.0	2.3	4.4	−0.7	−2.9	0.7	0.0	2.2	3.6	0.7	−6.9
Textile and products	2.1	2.7	4.7	0.6	0.6	−1.9	−1.1	−0.7	4.0	−1.3	2.6	0.6	−3.2
Leather and products	5.5	0.0	7.8	6.5	−1.5	6.2	−1.6	4.2	7.2	4.5	−0.8	5.5	−0.8
Silk deliveries	6.0	4.2	−4.1	2.8	5.5	−27.3	−39.3	−70.6	50.0	†	†	†	†
Rubber products	1.3	1.9	2.5	18.5	−20.3	−15.0	0.8	2.3	†	†	†	†	†
Manufactures, total	2.0	1.3	4.6	2.5	0.6	0.6	0.6	1.2	1.8	1.2	2.3	1.1	0.0
Nonferrous metals and products	3.5	2.2	3.3	−1.6	3.2	−1.6	1.6	3.6	2.7	1.6	0.5	−2.1	−3.2
Manufactured food products	0.8	1.7	0.0	3.3	−0.8	4.8	−1.5	3.1	5.2	2.8	2.2	0.7	−1.4
Paper and paper products	3.1	1.5	6.0	2.1	0.7	0.7	−2.0	1.4	4.8	1.3	−1.3	−2.6	
Petroleum and coal products	0.8	−1.6	3.3	1.6	0.8	1.6	1.5	0.8	1.5	3.0	−2.9	−3.0	
Fuels	7.1	−28.9	40.7	6.6	1.6	1.6	−0.8	0.8	0.8	−0.8	0.8	−2.3	−2.4
Metals	0.0	0.7	2.0	−0.7	0.0	−2.0	−2.0	0.7	0.7	4.1	−2.0	0.7	0.7

a Not available for publication separately.

SOURCE: Derived from data published in the *Federal Reserve Bulletin*.

Appendix I

TABLE 8
VALUE OF UNITED STATES EXPORTS BY QUARTERS
(In thousands of dollars.)

Exports	Year ending June, 1939	1939		1940				1941			
		Third quarter	Fourth quarter	First quarter	Second quarter	Third quarter	Fourth quarter	First quarter	Second quarter	Third quarter	Fourth quarter
All exports........	2,919,732	768,689	992,477	1,067,635	999,772	962,188	993,427	986,001	1,099,866	1,231,045	1,809,749
Europe............	1,228,429	322,616	395,184	498,431	409,580	380,114	357,027	336,341	367,851	445,357	†a
United Kingdom.	501,942	140,778	134,885	177,567	181,029	337,038	311,225	289,409	333,959	401,372	†
South America....	282,304	72,116	115,914	117,887	121,512	97,199	98,044	95,597	113,673	121,391	†

a Not available for separate publication.
SOURCE: *Survey of Current Business*.

TABLE 9
TOTAL STOCK OF MONEY
(In millions of dollars.)

1939

Demand deposits, adjusted (June 30)..................................	28,709
Deposits in Federal Reserve banks (June 28):	
U. S. Treasury general account................................	962
Foreign banks..	351
Outside currency..	6,005
	36,027

1940

Demand deposits, adjusted (June 29)..................................	33,542
Deposits in Federal Reserve banks (June 26):	
U. S. Treasury general account................................	301
Foreign banks..	659
Outside currency..	6,699
	41,201

1941

Demand deposits, adjusted..	38,192
Deposits in Federal Reserve banks (June 25):	
U. S. Treasury general account................................	1,081
Foreign banks..	1,240
Outside currency..	8,157
	48,670

Time deposits excluding domestic interbank

1939.......................................	25,803
1940.......................................	26,438
1941.......................................	26,939

Explanation of table 9.—The supply of money includes demand deposits adjusted, deposits of the U. S. Treasury and of foreign banks in the Federal Reserve banks, and outside currency. These three items are not always exactly comparable with respect to date, but the variation is only of one or two days. The calculations were carried out as follows. The deposits of the U. S. Treasury (U. S. Treasurer, general account) and of foreign governments in the Federal Reserve banks are obtainable directly from the *Federal Reserve Bulletin*. These two items are not usually included in the concept of the stock of money, but there is no reason for excluding them since they are drawn upon to make current expenditures. Circulating currency outside the Federal Reserve banks and Treasury is obtained from the *Federal Reserve Bulletin*, and from this figure it is necessary to subtract vault cash of all active banks as given in the annual reports of the Comptroller of the Currency. The resulting difference is outside currency. In order to obtain a figure of demand deposits adjusted, it is necessary to subtract the "float" from total demand deposits. Using the *Federal Reserve Bulletin*, one

Appendix I

can arrive immediately at member bank float by subtracting member bank demand deposits adjusted from member bank demand deposits exclusive of U. S. Government deposits and interbank deposits. (U. S. Government deposits and interbank deposits are not there included in demand deposits adjusted.) Thus one can express member bank float as a percentage of member bank gross demand deposits (this latter item includes all demand deposits except domestic interbank deposits). It was assumed that the float percentage would be the same for all banks as for member banks; therefore one can multiply the float percentage by the demand deposits of all active banks exclusive of domestic interbank deposits as obtained from the Comptroller's report. With this float figure it is possible to estimate demand deposits adjusted for all banks.

The foregoing methods were used for 1939 and 1940, but for 1941 the lack of availability of the Comptroller's report rendered it impossible to determine the precise amount of nonmember demand deposits. Since, however, total nonmember deposits remained almost unchanged from 1940 to 1941, we have assumed that the ratio of demand to total deposits also remained unchanged in the nonmember banks. Float was calculated in the same manner as for 1939 and 1940.

If the ratio of total income and of the stock of money thus derived is considered the income velocity for a calendar year, then it is implied that the stock of money as of June may be taken as the average stock of money during the year. If conditions in the weekly reporting member banks were "representative," the error in this procedure is small for the years under consideration.

TABLE 10
The Deficit of the Federal Government Including Its Agencies
(In millions of dollars.)

	Fiscal year ending		
	1939	1940	1941
Excess expenditures of the federal government......	3542	3611	5103
Excess receipts of federal agencies and trust accounts	890	136	− 148
	2652	3475	5251
Increase in holdings of government securities by the federal agencies and trust accounts.............	1109	1159	1413
	1543	2316	3838
Increase in outstanding, fully guaranteed securities (i.e., in securities issued by the federal agencies)....	597	48	862
Deficit..	2140	2364	4700

Source: *Federal Reserve Bulletin.*

Explanation of table 10.—The aggregate balance of the agencies should be added to the crude federal deficit if the balance is a deficit, or it should be subtracted if it is a surplus (as it was in the fiscal years 1939 and 1940). The resulting figure is not yet the deficit of the aggregate consisting of the federal government and of its agencies. In the accounts of the agencies, all their outlays, including those on government securities, appear as expenditures and the resulting figures are set against all their receipts, including those from borrowing. Adding the final deficit figures of the agencies to those of the federal government (or subtracting the surplus of the agencies from the federal deficit) results in a figure which is "too high" by the outlays of the agencies on federal securities, since these outlays are considered "expenditures" of the agencies without being classified as "revenues" of the federal government; and, on the other hand, the aggregate deficit figure arrived at by simple adding (or subtracting) is "too low" by the borrowing undertaken by the agencies, since this borrowing gives rise to "receipts" in their accounts, while the deficit should reflect the difference between expenditures and receipts other than those from borrowing. Hence the deficit figure arrived at by lumping together the "excess" figures of the government with those of the agencies should be further corrected by subtracting the outlays of the agencies on federal securities and by adding the borrowing undertaken by the agencies. The figure thus derived may be viewed as the deficit of the federal government in the broader sense, that is, as the deficit of an aggregate consisting of the federal government and of its agencies. The same figure may also be derived by correcting the new borrowing of the "aggregate" for changes in the general fund balance (see footnote, p. 70).

Appendix I

TABLE 11
Percentage Increase over the Corresponding Month of the Preceding Year in Retail Sales (Current Prices)

Month	Department store sales, total U. S. (adjusted)	Grocery chain store (adjusted)	U. S. rural sales of general merchandise (adjusted)
1940			
June	5.8	11.9	4.6
July	5.7	12.7	5.8
August	11.4	11.2	11.4
September	7.8	2.7	1.9
October	2.2	5.1	— 1.1
November	7.5	5.8	12.4
December	6.3	7.7	10.3
1941			
January	9.8	12.2	8.3
February	14.4	10.1	14.0
March	15.7	13.7	9.0
April	16.9	15.0	31.7
May	18.0	14.8	20.9
June	14.3	20.2	18.5
July	25.0	21.6	34.5
August	36.7	24.4	42.9
September	19.6	25.2	36.1
October	11.7	29.8	36.6
November	16.0	28.4	35.5
December	9.9	29.8	23.3
1942			
January	36.6	37.0	36.6
February	22.3	30.9	23.9
March	20.4	—[a]	42.0

[a] New series begins (back data not yet available).
Source: Data published in the *Survey of Current Business*.

APPENDIX II: CHARTS

RELATING TO TOTAL LABOR-HOUR INPUT AND PHYSICAL OUTPUT IN SPECIFIC INDUSTRIES

(See page 46 of text)

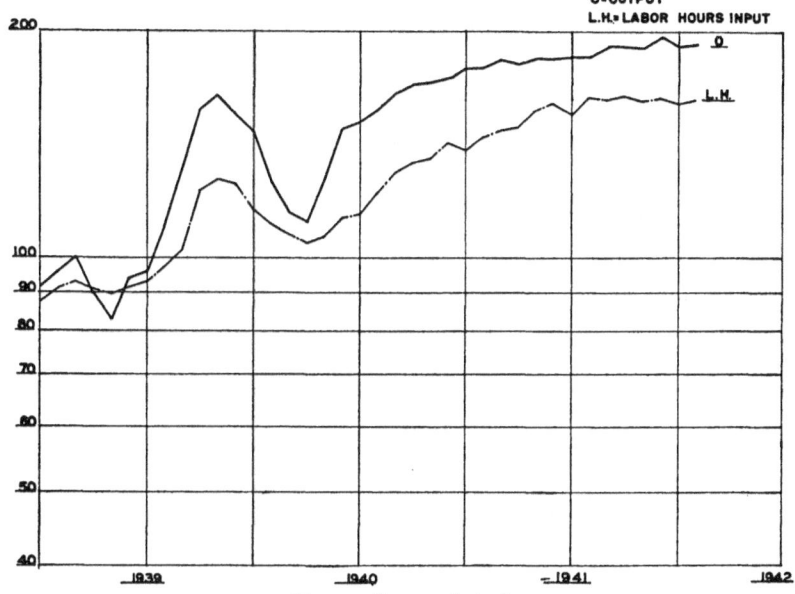

Chart 1. Iron and steel.

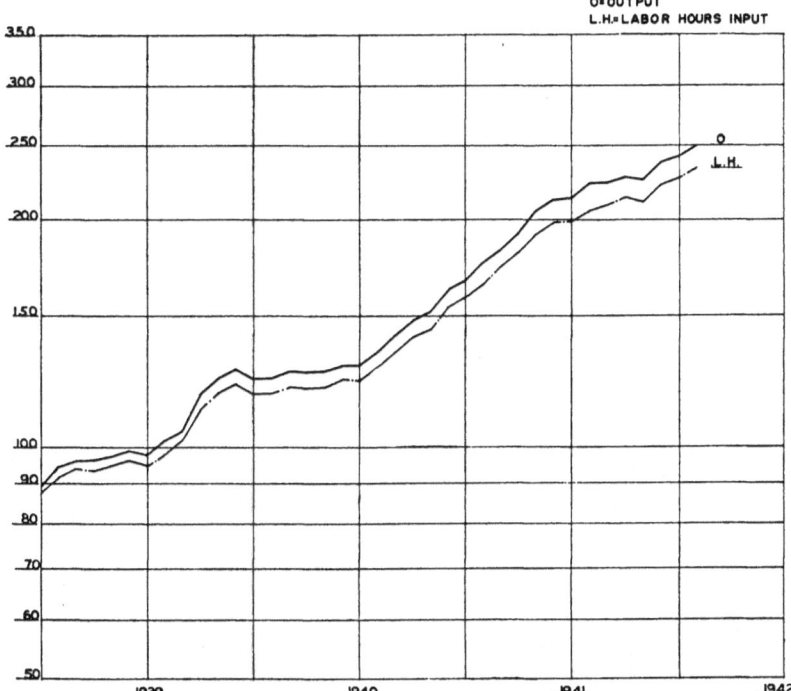

Chart 2. Machinery.

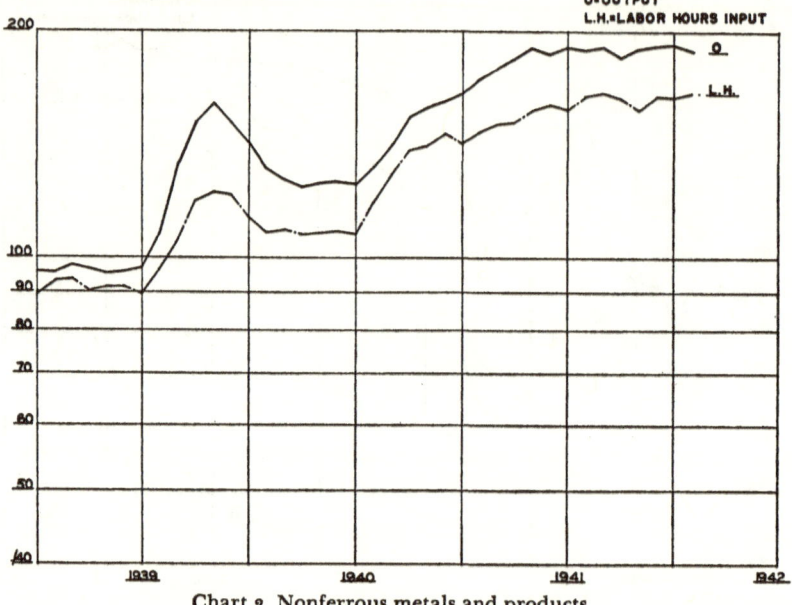

Chart 3. Nonferrous metals and products.

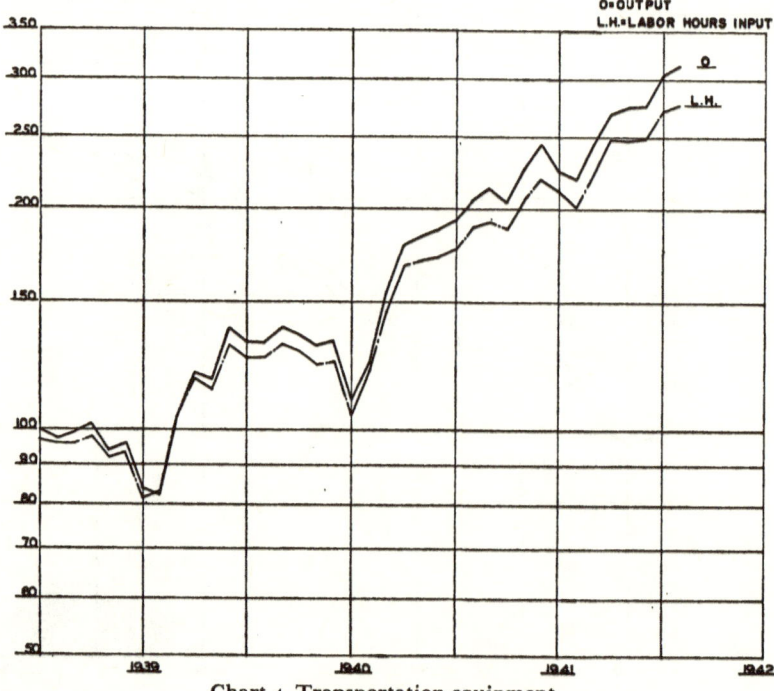

Chart 4. Transportation equipment.

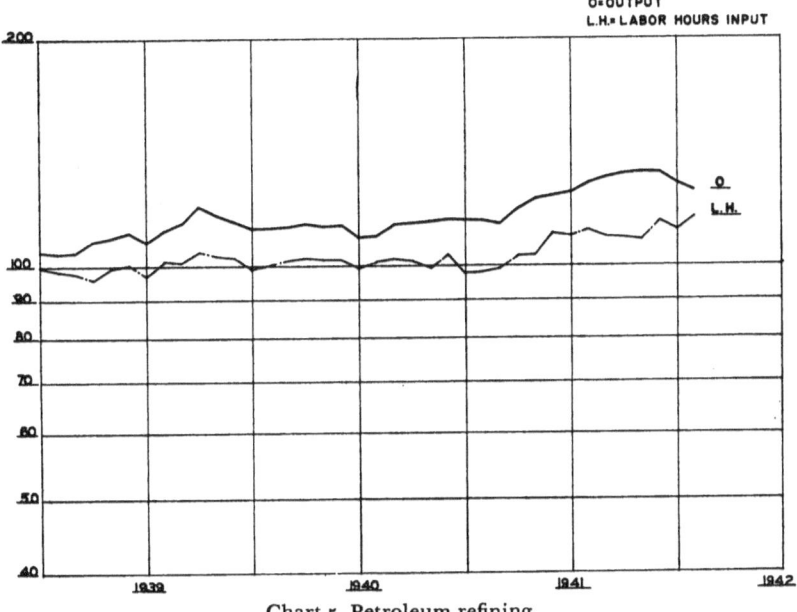

Chart 5. Petroleum refining.

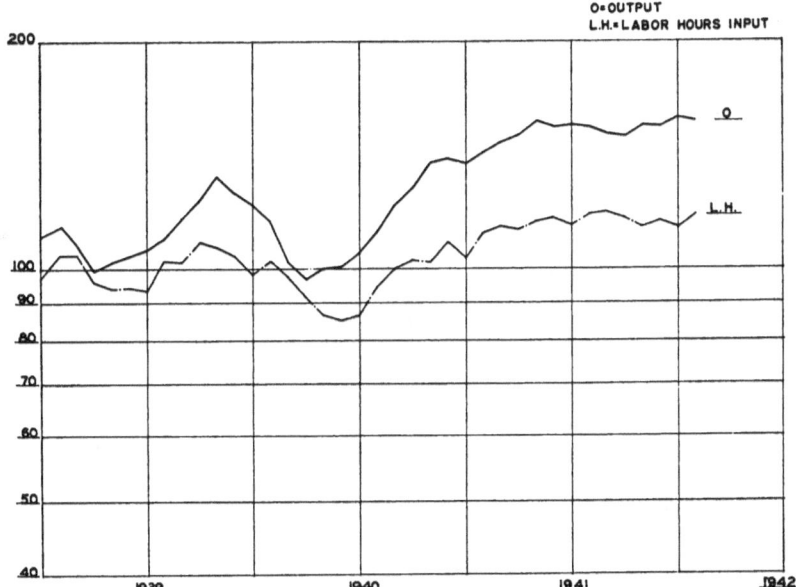

Chart 6. Textiles and products.

Publications Used

ALTMAN, OSCAR L. Temporary National Economic Committee, Monograph No. 37: *Saving, Investment and National Income*. Washington: Government Printing Office, 1941.

ANGELL, JAMES W. "Taxation, Inflation and the Defense Program," *Review of Economic Statistics*, May, 1941.

———. *The Behavior of Money*. New York: McGraw-Hill, 1936.

———. *Investment and Business Cycles*. New York: McGraw-Hill, 1941.

BALOGH, THOMAS. "The Drift Towards a Rational Foreign Exchange Policy," *Economica*, August, 1940.

BANGS, R. B. "The Changing Relation of Consumer Income and Expenditure," *Survey of Current Business*, April, 1942.

BANK FOR INTERNATIONAL SETTLEMENTS. *11th Annual Report*, 1941.

BAYKOV, A. "Experience in the Organization of War Economy in the USSR," *Economic Journal*, December, 1941.

BENEDICT, M. R. "The Control of Post War Deflation," *Bank of America Business Review*, June, 1942.

BLAKEY, ROY G. AND GLADYS C. *The Federal Income Tax*. New York: Longmans, Green, 1940.

BOARD OF GOVERNORS OF THE FEDERAL RESERVE SYSTEM. *Federal Reserve Bulletin*, 1939–1942.

BRESCIANI-TURRONI, CONSTANTINO. *The Economics of Inflation: A Study of Currency Depreciation in Post-War Germany*. London: Allen and Unwin, 1937.

BROWN UNIVERSITY ECONOMISTS. *Introduction to War Economics*. Chicago: Irwin, 1942.

CLARK, COLIN. *National Income and Outlay*. London: Macmillan, 1937.

CLARK, JOHN M. "Further Remarks on Defense Financing and Inflation," *Review of Economic Statistics*, August, 1941.

———. *The Costs of the World War to the American People*. New Haven: Yale Univ. Press, 1931.

COLM, GERHARD, AND TARASOV, HELEN. Temporary National Economic Committee, Monograph No. 3: *Who Pays the Taxes?* Washington: Government Printing Office, 1940.

COMMAND PAPER 6261 [BRITISH]. *An Analysis of the Sources of War Finance and an Estimate of National Income and Expenditure in 1938 and 1940*. London, 1941.

COMPTROLLER OF THE CURRENCY. *Seventy-Seventh Annual Report Covering the Year Ended October 31, 1940*. Washington: Government Printing Office, 1941.

———. *Seventy-Eighth Annual Report Covering the Year Ended October 31, 1941*. Washington: Government Printing Office, 1942.

CONE, FREDERICK M. *Monthly Income Payments in the United States, 1929–40*. United States Department of Commerce, Bureau of Foreign and Domestic Commerce. Washington, 1940.

COPELAND, MORRIS A. "Production Planning for a War Economy," *Annals of the American Academy of Political and Social Science*, March, 1942.

CURRIE, LAUCHLIN B. *The Supply and Control of Money in the United States.* Cambridge: Harvard Univ. Press, 1935.

Defense (later *Victory*): Official Weekly Bulletin of the Agencies in the Office for Emergency Management. Washington, 1941–1942.

DEPARTMENT OF COMMERCE. "Effect of Russian Campaign on German Economy," *Foreign Commerce Weekly*, November 8, 1941.

———. "Germany's Limitation of Dividends," *Foreign Commerce Weekly*, August 16, 1941.

Economist, The. London, 1939–1942.

ELLIS, HOWARD S. "Some Fundamentals in the Theory of Velocity," *Quarterly Journal of Economics*, May, 1938.

GALBRAITH, J. K. "The Selection and Timing of Inflation Controls," *Review of Economic Statistics*, May, 1941.

GILBERT, MILTON. "War Expenditures and National Production," *Survey of Current Business*, Bureau of Foreign and Domestic Commerce, Department of Commerce, March, 1942.

GILBERT, MILTON, AND BANGS, R. B. "Preliminary Estimates of Gross National Product, 1929–41," *Survey of Current Business*, Bureau of Foreign and Domestic Commerce, Department of Commerce, May, 1942.

GILBERT, MILTON, AND YNTEMA, DWIGHT B. "National Income Exceeds 76 Billion Dollars in 1940," *Survey of Current Business*, Bureau of Foreign and Domestic Commerce, Department of Commerce, June, 1941.

GRETHER, E. T., AND DAVISSON, M. "Price Fixing versus Tax Policy," *Annals of the American Academy of Political and Social Science*, March, 1941.

HANSEN, ALVIN H. "Defense Financing and Inflation Potentialities," *Review of Economic Statistics*, February, 1941.

———. *Fiscal Policy and Business Cycles.* New York: Norton, 1941.

———. "Income, Consumption and National Defense," *Yale Review*, Autumn, 1941.

———. "Some Additional Comments on the Inflation Symposium," *Review of Economic Statistics*, May, 1941.

HARRIS, SEYMOUR E. *The Economics of American Defense.* New York: Norton, 1941.

HART, A. G. "Use of Flexible Taxes to Combat Inflation," *American Economic Review*, March, 1942.

———. "Safeguards Against Inflation," *Review of Economic Statistics*, May, 1941.

HART, A. G., ALLEN, E. D., ET AL. *Paying for Defense.* Philadelphia: Blakiston, 1941.

HICKS, J. R., HICKS, V. K., AND ROSTAS, L. *The Taxation of War Wealth.* Oxford: Clarendon Press, 1941.

INTERNATIONAL REFERENCE SERVICE. *The British Exchequer Returns for 1940–41 and the Budget for the Year Ending March 1942.* Bureau of Foreign and Domestic Commerce, Department of Commerce.

———. *Price Control in Germany: Policy and Technique,* Bureau of Foreign and Domestic Commerce, Department of Commerce, April, 1941.

Publications Used 175

INTERNATIONAL REFERENCE SERVICE, HENRY CHALMERS. *Impact of the War upon the Trade Policies of Foreign Countries.* Bureau of Foreign and Domestic Commerce, Department of Commerce, March, 1941.

JACOBSTEIN, MEYER, AND MOULTON, HAROLD G. *Effects of the Defense Program on Prices, Wages, and Profits.* Washington: Brookings Institution, September 30, 1941.

KALDOR, N. "The White Paper on National Income and Expenditure," *Economic Journal*, June–September, 1941.

KALECKI, M. *Bulletin,* Institute of Statistics, Oxford, Vol. 3, No. 8, June 7, 1941.

KEYNES, J. M. "The Income and Fiscal Potential of Great Britain," *Economic Journal*, December, 1939.

———. "The Concept of National Income," *Economic Journal*, March, 1940.

———. *How to Pay for the War: a Radical Plan for the Chancellor of the Exchequer.* New York: Harcourt, Brace, 1940.

KNOTT, GRACE W. *Estimated Distribution of Civilian Expenditures, 1940, 1941, and 1942.* Office of Production Management, Bureau of Research and Statistics, July, 1941.

KOVACS, L. "An Installment Plan for Post-War Deliveries," *Economic Journal*, December, 1941.

KUZNETS, SIMON. *National Income and Its Composition, 1919–1938.* New York: National Bureau of Economic Research, 1941.

———. *National Income and Capital Formation 1919–1935: A Preliminary Report.* New York: National Bureau of Economic Research, 1937.

———. *Commodity Flow and Capital Formation in the Recent Recovery and Decline.* Bulletin No. 74 of the National Bureau of Economic Research, 1939.

MAIZELS, ALFRED. "Consumption, Investment and National Expenditure in Wartime," *Economica*, May, 1941.

MELLON, H. J. "German Stock Purchases as an Inflation Hedge," *Conference Board Economic Record*, National Industrial Conference Board, October 24, 1941.

NATHAN, OTTO. "Consumption in Germany During the Period of Rearmament," *Quarterly Journal of Economics*, May, 1942.

NATIONAL CITY BANK OF NEW YORK. *Monthly Reports,* 1941–1942.

NATIONAL INDUSTRIAL CONFERENCE BOARD, INC. *Economic Record,* 1939–1942.

NATIONAL RESOURCES COMMITTEE. *Consumer Incomes in the United States: Their Distribution in 1935–36.* Washington: Government Printing Office, 1938.

———. *Consumer Expenditures in the United States: Estimates for 1935–36.* Washington: Government Printing Office, 1939.

———. *Family Expenditures in the United States: Statistical Tables and Appendixes.* Washington: Government Printing Office, 1941.

New York Times, 1941 and 1942.

NIXON, RUSSELL A., AND SAMUELSON, PAUL A. "Estimates of Unemployment in the United States," *Review of Economic Statistics,* August, 1940.

PIGOU, A. C. *The Economics of Welfare.* London: Macmillan, 1929.

———. *Political Economy of War.* London: Macmillan, 1940.

———. "Types of War Inflation," *Economic Journal,* December, 1941.

POOLE, KENYON E. *German Taxation under a System of Controlled Production and Rationing.* Washington: National Tax Association, 1941.

RECONSTRUCTION FINANCE CORPORATION. *Information Concerning Loans and Purchases to Aid in the National-Defense Program.* Circular No. 23, January, 1942.

———. *Report to the President and the Congress of the United States.* Washington, January 18, 1941, May 9, 1941, and March 21, 1942.

RICHARDSON, J. HENRY. "Consumer Rationing in Great Britain," *Canadian Journal of Economics and Political Science,* February, 1942.

SECOND FEDERAL RESERVE DISTRICT. *Monthly Review of Credit and Business Conditions,* 1941–1942.

SEIDEMANN, HENRY P. *Curtailment of Non-Defense Expenditures.* Washington: Brookings Institution, December 29, 1941.

SHOUP, CARL. "Choice of Tax Measure to Avert Inflation," *Review of Economic Statistics,* May, 1941.

SIEGEL, IRVING H. "Hourly Earnings and Unit Labor Cost in Manufacturing," *Journal of the American Statistical Association,* September, 1940.

SINGER, H. W. "The German War Economy in the Light of Economic Periodicals," *Economic Journal,* December, 1940, April, 1941, September, 1941, December, 1941, April, 1942.

SLICHTER, SUMNER H. "The Conditions of Expansion," *American Economic Review,* March, 1942.

SPIEGEL, HENRY WILLIAM. *The Economics of Total War.* New York: Appleton-Century, 1942.

STEIN, EMANUEL, AND BACKMAN, JULES. *War Economics.* New York: Farrar and Rinehart, 1942.

TAX INSTITUTE [SYMPOSIUM]. *Financing the War.* Philadelphia: University of Pennsylvania, 1942.

UNITED STATES BUREAU OF THE BUDGET. *The Budget of the United States Government for the Fiscal Year Ending June 30, 1942.* Washington: Government Printing Office, 1941.

UNITED STATES BUREAU OF THE CENSUS, DEPARTMENT OF COMMERCE. *Population, Preliminary Figures on Employment Status, Series P-4.*

UNITED STATES BUREAU OF THE CENSUS, DEPARTMENT OF COMMERCE. *Biennial Census of Manufactures, 1937.* Washington: Government Printing Office, 1939.

UNITED STATES DEPARTMENT OF COMMERCE, BUREAU OF FOREIGN AND DOMESTIC COMMERCE. *Survey of Current Business,* Washington, 1939–1942.

UNITED STATES DEPARTMENT OF LABOR, BUREAU OF LABOR STATISTICS. *Productivity and Unit Labor Cost in Selected Manufacturing Industries 1919–1940.* Washington, February, 1942.

UNITED STATES OFFICE OF PRODUCTION MANAGEMENT. *Financing Defense Projects,* Bulletins Nos. 1, 2, and 3, December 1, 1941.

UNITED STATES TREASURY DEPARTMENT. *Monthly Bulletin,* Washington, 1941 and 1942.

Publications Used

VILLARD, HENRY HILGARD. *Deficit Spending and the National Income.* New York: Farrar and Rinehart, 1941.

VOZNESENDKY, N. *Economic Results of USSR in 1940 and the Plan of National Economic Development for 1941.* USSR Government Press, 1941.

WERNETTE, J. PHILIP. "Financing the Defense Program," *American Economic Review*, December, 1941.

ZVEREV, COMMISSAR FOR FINANCE. *Budget of the USSR for 1941.* Report at the 8th Session of the Supreme Soviet, February, 1941.

Index

Allen, E. D., 101, 105
Angell, James W., 76, 76 n.
Anti-Inflation Bill, 150

Bangs, R. B., 42, 125 n.
Benedict, M. R., 126 n.

Canada, 16, 16 n., 149
Capital consumption, estimates of, 43, 134
Capital formation, estimates of, 26, 26 n., 28, 28 n., 35, 35 n., 60, 153
Ceilings on prices and wages. *See* General Maximum Price Regulation and Anti-Inflation Bill
Compulsory lending, 11, 96–99, 107, 113–114, 126 n., 132, 132 n., 148–149
Congress, U. S., 100–101, 120–121, 122 n., 148–150
Consumer's credit, 9, 123 n., 126, 126 n.
Consumption, estimates of, 35, 42–43, 48, 50, 58, 73, 136
Consumption taxes, 12–14, 88–89, 90–91, 106, 122, 129, 133, 141–146, 149
Corporate earnings, 93, 93 n.
Corporate taxes, 6, 11–12, 93, 107, 116–119, 122, 132, 132 n., 149
Cost-plus contracts, 18 n., 123 n.

Defense financing, techniques of, 68 n.
Defense loans, 70, 70 n.
Defense Plant Corporation, 68 n.
Deficit, estimates of, 20, 67–69, 72, 122, 134–135, 160
Deficit, fiscal, 20, 20 n., 67, 69, 70 n., 72–73, 120, 127, 134–135, 137
Deficit, method of computing for U.S., 160
Dirks, Fr. C., 27, 27 n.
Durable-goods expenditures, estimates of, 27, 57, 124–125, 153

Emergency Price Control Act, 123 n.
Employment, estimates of, 29, 30, 30 n., 44, 46, 152
Excess-profits tax. *See* Corporate taxes
Excess reserves, 85–86
Exchequer, British, 132–136

Exemptions (income tax), 101, 103, 106, 121, 140–142, 148
Exports, 67, 157

Farm prices, 18 n., 64, 123, 123 n., 150
General Maximum Price Regulation (American), 16, 123 n., 131
Germany, 16, 137
Gilbert, Milton, 25 n., 26 n., 27 n., 41 n., 42, 42 n., 43 n., 125 n.
Gold influx, 71, 73
Great Britain, 16, 50 n., 67, 132–136, 140, 142–143, 149

Hart, Albert G., 101, 105

Incentives, economic, 9, 10, 12, 92–93, 113, 116–118
Income, distribution of, 102–104
Income tax, withholding of, at source, 4, 11 n., 107–109, 140, 148
Income-tax exemption. *See* Exemptions
Income-tax rates, individual, 104, 121–122, 140, 148–150; *see also* Tax revenues
Inflation, concept of, 2 n., 110, 129
Inflation controls, effectiveness of, 17–19, 126–128, 130–131, 135–136, 138
Inflationary gap, 14, 17, 20, 124, 126, 140
Italy, 16

Japan, 16, 22

Kalecki, M., 17 n., 128
Keynes, J. M., 11 n., 25, 96
Knott, Grace W., 25 n.
Kuznets, Simon, 24 n., 28 n.

Labor allocation, 59, 123, 123 n., 124
Lend-Lease Act, 67, 134, 136–137
Local taxation, 150 n.

Marginal efficiency of capital, 25
Marginal tax rate, 10–12, 104, 113–119, 121–122, 149–150

[179]

Marginal utility, 34–35
Money stock, estimates of, 4, 66, 77, 85, 135, 158–159
Morgenthau, Henry, Jr., Secretary of the Treasury, 58, 120–121
Mosk, S. A., 4 n.
Multiplier effect, 25, 31, 68

National income, concepts of, 41–42, 99 n.
National income, estimates of, 4, 24, 24 n., 25, 25 n., 41–42, 99, 133, 133 n., 153
National Resources Committee, 57, 102–103, 105 n.
Nelson, Donald M., chairman, War Production Board, 150

Office of Price Administration (O.P.A.), 75, 93 n., 102
Office of Production Management (O.P.M.), 41, 57
Ophelimity, 88

Pareto, Vilfredo, 88
Parity prices, 18 n., 123, 123 n., 150
Pigou, A. C., 42 n., 48, 49 n.
Postwar credit. See Compulsory lending
Price-level, estimates of, 29, 64, 136, 155
Price movements, relative, 8, 64, 90, 146–147, 150
Priorities, 6, 16, 36, 64, 123 n., 130
Production, ban on, 125, 125 n.
Production, estimates of, 29, 29 n., 30–33, 44, 46–47, 49, 84, 151, 156, Appendix II: Charts
Public debt, 38–39, 138
Purchases Tax (British), 143 n.

Quality, deterioration of, 18, 129

Reconstruction Finance Corporation, 22, 23 n., 68, 72
Regulation W (of Federal Reserve Board), 126 n.
Retail sales, 161
Robertson, D. H., 127
Rolph, E. R., 4 n.
Russia, 137

Samuelson, Paul A., 30 n.
Savings, 3 n., 5, 19, 20, 62 n., 96, 124–125, 125 n., 131
Savings, corporate, 5–7, 92, 94–95, 125
Smith, Harold D., U. S. Budget Director, 58, 150
Social Security taxes, 96, 100, 120, 132, 148
State and local taxes, 150 n.

Tax revenues, estimates of, 24 n., 89, 91, 93, 99, 104, 107, 120–121, 132–133, 148–150
Terborgh, George, 27, 27 n.
Textile industry, output and labor hours, 47
Thomas, Brinley, 136, 136 n.
Treasury, U. S., 3, 7, 16, 23 n., 62–63, 86, 93, 96, 100, 103, 105, 108–109, 121–122, 139, 148–149

Unemployment, estimates of, 30, 30 n.
United Nations, 67

Velocity of circulation, 74–77, 77 n., 95, 128
Victory levy, 148

Wages, estimates of, 32–33, 154
War (defense) spending, estimates of, 4, 8, 23, 35, 40, 58, 67, 72–73, 150
Wicksell, Kunt, 129
World War I, 17, 145

www.ingramcontent.com/pod-product-compliance
Lightning Source LLC
Chambersburg PA
CBHW021709230426
43668CB00008B/772